Using Brainpower
in the Classroom

This book offers a realistic, practical and accessible model to allow teachers to incorporate the best of recent brain-based research into their teaching. Its five steps involve: making learning multi-sensory, ensuring activities match the dominant intelligences of the learners, matching types of learning to the gender of the pupils, using the lesson structure to fit the natural attention span of the brain, and managing the classroom environment to make it brain-friendly and active in supporting learning. Illustrated throughout with classroom examples from a wide range of subject areas, the book is highly practical in focus and the ideas it contains can easily be adapted to work with all age ranges and types of school.

Steve Garnett is Senior Manager at a UK comprehensive school, he is also an experienced training provider delivering training in the Primary, Secondary and Independent sectors across Nottinghamshire, to teachers representing over 300 schools.

Using Brainpower in the Classroom

Five steps to accelerate learning

Steve Garnett

Routledge
Taylor & Francis Group

LONDON AND NEW YORK

First published 2005
by Routledge
2 Park Square, Milton Park, Abingdon, Oxon OX14 4RN

Simultaneously published in the USA and Canada
by Routledge
270 Madison Ave, New York NY 10016

Routledge is an imprint of the Taylor & Francis Group

© 2005 Steve Garnett

Typeset in Times New Roman by
Florence Production Ltd, Stoodleigh, Devon
Printed and bound in Great Britain by
TJ International Ltd, Padstow, Cornwall

British Library Cataloguing in Publication Data
A catalogue record for this book is available from the
British Library

Library of Congress Cataloging in Publication Data
A catalog record for this book has been requested

ISBN 0–415–34382–8 (hbk)
ISBN 0–415–34383–6 (pbk)

Contents

Illustrations

Figures

Boxes

Everything should be made as simple
as possible, but not simpler.
                                Albert Einstein

Introduction

No one was talking about how the brain functions during learning when I was a trainee teacher in the late 1980s. The reason for this is that around 80 per cent of what we know about how the brain functions has only been learned in the last fifteen to twenty years. Indeed the US Congress described the 1990s as the 'Decade of the Brain'. Now much of this new knowledge is coming from developments and research in neurological and behavioural science. Our increasing knowledge is also being helped considerably by developments in brain scanning techniques, which is giving us a greater understanding of how the brain processes knowledge and how and where it functions when we learn. We need to understand the potential impact of this on our work in the classroom. In particular, how it can help our pupils become even more engaged, motivated and challenged.

However, one of the problems is that there is such a huge amount of information available for teachers interested in brain-based learning and its application to the classroom. It's difficult to know where to look and where to begin. For example an internet hunt for articles related to 'brain-based learning' through the search engine 'Google', came up with 1,670,000 results! Also, experience from training teachers in brain-based learning techniques has suggested the need for a book that distils and demystifies this knowledge and demonstrates how to apply it in a typical classroom situation. Teachers need something that is clear, realistic and that can be used in the classroom immediately. The purpose of this book then is to provide a resource for teachers that utilises some of the best of what the internet has to offer, together with an overview of the theory and research behind the development of whole brain learning and, in turn, accelerated learning. This book aims to do this by breaking down the issues involved in using the brain and accelerated learning issues into five steps, which are:

Learning
Cognition
Gender
Whole lesson
Physical environment

Each step has a chapter devoted to it. Each chapter begins by offering an overview of the relevant 'Theoretical background' within the context of emerging knowledge of the brain. This section is designed to provide a theoretical backdrop to the practical ideas that follow in the section 'In the classroom'. This is the part that guides the teacher into how to apply the theory into classroom practice. It is full of case studies and practical ideas. Although it draws on a range of subjects to provide examples, the reader should be encouraged to see how each idea can be applied to their own subject. Then for the reader who is keen to develop an even deeper understanding, the section 'Where next?' offers further reading.

The thrust of the book is to provide a practical handbook for teachers who still want an overview of the research, but more importantly a rich and varied repertoire of ideas to put into practice in their own classroom.

*   *   *

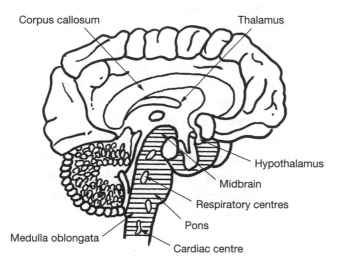

Figure 0.1 The anatomy of the brain

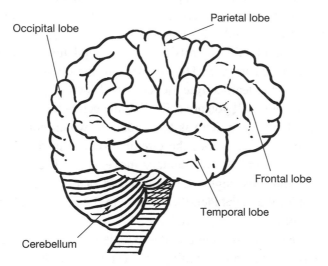

Figure 0.2 The anatomy of the brain

With a title such as 'Using Brainpower in the Classroom' it is perhaps logical to begin with an overview of the anatomy of the brain. This will help develop an understanding of why it is so important to use the whole brain, rather than certain parts, in the quest to accelerate the process of learning in the classroom.

The brain is the most complex part of the body. Imagine all the people in the world sending each other a message at the same time and this is still less than the number of processes the brain absorbs in one second! Weighing about three pounds and washed by protective fluid, the brain is the crown jewel of the human body. The brain is like a committee of experts. All parts of the brain work together, but each part has its own special properties.

For ease of understanding it is simpler to imagine the brain split into three sections:

> Hindbrain
> Midbrain
> Forebrain

The hindbrain includes the upper part of the spinal cord, the brain stem (an area approximately 3 inches long and including the medulla oblongata and pons (shown in Figure 0.1)) and the cerebellum. The hindbrain controls the body's vital functions such as respiration and heart rate. The cerebellum coordinates movement and is involved in learned rote movements. When playing the piano or hitting a tennis ball you are activating the cerebellum. The uppermost part of the brain stem is the midbrain, which controls some reflex actions and is part of the circuit involved in the control of eye movements and other voluntary movements. The forebrain is the largest and most highly developed part of the human brain. It consists of all the lobes identified in Figure 0.2, collectively known as the cerebrum.

This area is usually the one that people notice most when they see pictures of the brain. Sitting at the top of the brain it is the source of intellectual activities. It holds your memories, allows you to plan, allows you to imagine and to think. It allows you to recognise friends, read books and play games.

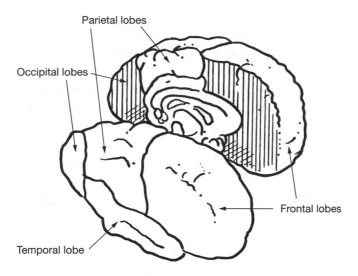

Figure 0.3 Two hemispheres of the brain

These lobes identified in Figure 0.3 all process different functions:

- Frontal lobe – awareness, memory, attention and concentration, cognition, motivation, judgement, voluntary movement, expressive language, emotional control, impulse control, word associations, following instructions, decision-making, personality, assigning meanings to words we choose.
- Parietal lobe – visual attention, awareness of spatial relationships, touch, recognition of faces, manipulation of objects, integration of different senses that allows for understanding a single concept.
- Occipital lobe – visual perception, visual input, reading, movement of eyes.
- Temporal lobe – hearing, music, receptive language, comprehension of language, memory acquisition, memory of non-verbal events, information retrieval, categorisation of objects, expressed behaviour.

Nobel Prize winning work by Roger Sperry in the 1970s increased our understanding of the make up of the cerebrum (see Figure 0.3). He developed the notion of hemispheric dominance for certain functions within it.

The cerebrum is split into two halves (hemispheres) by a deep fissure. Despite this split, the two cerebral hemispheres communicate with each other through a thick tract of nerve fibres that lies at the base of this fissure (corpus callosum). Although the two hemispheres seem to be mirror images of each other, they are different. Figure 0.4 offers a useful checklist.

Coating the surface of the cerebrum and cerebellum is a vital layer of thin tissue. It is called the neo-cortex. The word cortex is from the Latin word for bark, a metaphor to describe the outer layer. It is also the newest part of the brain, hence neo. Only latterly, in evolutionary terms, has the brain developed this part, and it's this that puts us at the top of the evolutionary 'tree'. This 'new

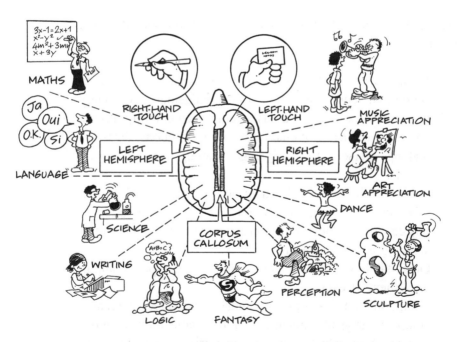

Figure 0.4 How the brain divides its work: cognitive functions of the left and right hemispheres

brain' is seen as broadly the part of the brain where higher order thinking takes place. In essence, it is the part that separates us from our closest evolutionary cousin, the chimpanzee.

Deep within the brain, hidden from view, are the structures that act as the gatekeepers between the spinal cord and the cerebrum. These structures control our emotional state and also modify our perceptions and responses depending on that state. Broadly described as the Limbic system, it includes areas such as the hypothalamus (the area that gets you up in the morning, gets adrenaline flowing, makes you feel exhilarated, angry or unhappy). Near here is the thalamus, a major clearing house for information going to and from the spinal cord and the cerebrum.

* * *

Which parts of this should interest us then? Well, we now know that different parts of the brain process different cognitive functions. So, if we want our pupils to use all of their brain during learning, we have to offer a repertoire of activities that involves among other things, logic, number, words, language, colour, music, movement and image.

This becomes critical for two reasons. First, we will see in the next chapter that all pupils have a preferred way of learning. What this means is that if teachers don't vary classroom activities they will not reach all parts of the brain. This will then disadvantage some pupils. Indeed, pupils learn more effectively if they learn in their preferred way.

The second is that pupils' understanding is developed, reinforced and increased if it is approached using a variety of stimuli, for example, words, pictures and actions. Think of learning to drive a car. If we just read a manual we wouldn't learn as effectively as if we used a combination of action (driving lessons), instruction (driving instructor) and reading the manual.

From work done in the field of psychology, we know that the different personality types that we encounter as teachers require different types of activities to access their dominant personality type. There is growing evidence, too, that we all have a preferred modality to receive information either through our Visual, Auditory or Kinaesthetic (VAK) senses. Therefore, we should now be offering opportunities to cater for a variety of preferred modalities. We also have a deeper understanding of the optimum conditions in which the brain can work. These include movement, water, music and the visual environment.

As well as this, there is a growing body of evidence that we all have a dominant intelligence. Despite the fact that some commentators argue that they are better described as competencies, the reality for teachers is that, again, we have to cater for a variety of needs in the classroom. Our pupils will have a dominant intelligence that could either be linguistic, logical/mathematical, interpersonal, intrapersonal, musical, visual/spatial, kinaesthetic, naturalistic or, indeed, existential. Again, the teacher will need to draw on a repertoire of activities to ensure all pupils not only learn in their dominant intelligence, but also, that their weaker intelligences are challenged too. The level of cognitive challenge we offer pupils also needs to reflect the kind of learner we teach. It is possible to set a hierarchy of cognitive challenges for our pupils. These allow them all to be challenged and for all of them to achieve.

We also have a better understanding of how to deliver learning to boys and girls that takes account of biological and neurological differences. By recognising the differences boys and girls undoubtedly have, we can manipulate the activities done in lessons to support the strengths of both kinds of learners and also develop their weaknesses too.

Our increasing knowledge of the natural attention cycle of the brain is demonstrating the importance of focusing on the 'whole lesson'. Creating informed and interesting starts to lessons utilises the time when the brain is naturally at its most receptive. Concentrating too on delivering a discrete activity at the end of learning, ensures that we make best use of the way the brain naturally remembers. Similarly, our increasing knowledge of how the memory works is suggesting the need to develop the use of the visual intelligence much more fully in learning, as well as other strategies to improve the ability to recall learning for future use.

Teachers can also use the classroom environment much more effectively to make it become our silent 'helper'. By paying attention to layout, lighting, heating, display, colour and music we can support our efforts in accelerating the process of learning.

How the brain learns

Finally, we now know what is actually happening in the brain when we learn. Any explanation is complex and so to make it more easily understood there is a danger of being over simplistic and, as a result, inaccurate. But essentially what happens is described in the next paragraph.

We have approximately 100 billion brain cells called neurons. When the brain is exposed to a stimulating experience the neurons connect with each other. If this kind of stimulating experience is sustained then the connections between neurons are strengthened. If we can subject our students to lots of high stimulus material and challenge in lessons then more neurons will connect and so increase learning. The stronger the connection between the neurons, the more effective and lasting the learning will be. The strengthening is done by revisiting the learning, reinforcing it and demonstrating that you know. When there are lots of connections, networks are then established. When this happens the learning is hard-wired to the brain and so it becomes very difficult to 'un-learn' the learning. Learning, then, can be defined as the establishment of these new networks, where before there weren't any.

To sum up it's helpful to know that:

- Every individual brain is different and immensely powerful – enough neurons to store 1,000 CD-ROMs, each one containing the Encarta encyclopaedia. So don't worry, pupils can't complain that their brains are full!
- We only use a fraction of our brain's true capacity (estimates range from 2 per cent to 10 per cent). Therefore there is huge capacity for increase.

- All brains suffer in a low sensory environment, in which the brain literally shrinks.
- We all prefer to learn in different ways and tapping into those individual experiences is essential for students to reach their potential.
- Of all the types of intelligences/competencies we have (originally seven were identified), our dominant intelligences are different, requiring different types of tasks.
- Intelligence is not fixed at birth but rather develops through experience and learning.
- Emotional experience is a crucial ingredient in learning. Emotions literally act as the 'gatekeeper' to learning.
- Motivation is a crucial part of learning.
- Fear and stress make learning impossible.
- Challenge, change and learning through mistakes are key factors in developing intelligence.
- Music can enhance the learning state.
- Right and left hemispheres of the cerebrum broadly process different types of information in different ways. Variety of activity allows you to utilise the whole brain.

*   *   *

Teachers want to make the most of this new knowledge about brain function but it has to be set within the context in which they work. We have to be cautious about the changes we should expect teachers to make. Schools, and indeed teachers, have to operate within the structures that are placed on them. The time of day when pupils are asked to learn, the environment they have to learn in, the structure of the curriculum, the prescribed method of delivery, the amount of time an individual teacher sees a class and the resources at their disposal, all of these can mitigate against effective learning.

*   *   *

Therefore, any proposed model should be based on this reality and also be persuasive, easily understood, highly practical and achievable. The choice of five steps in the subtitle of this book is deliberate. Most people can only ever remember about five concepts simultaneously. So by basing the model on five steps, teachers will have an easily remembered checklist.

'Whole brain' teaching and learning simply means using what knowledge we have about where and how the brain functions during learning and then applying this knowledge to our work in the classroom. Simply by approaching the process of learning differently we can use this knowledge to our pupils' advantage. The focus of this book is to offer a method to create a learning experience for your students that engages and motivates, which then builds the networks of neurons allowing learning to take place.

For this to develop further and for learning to accelerate, attention has also to be paid to the way your students like to learn, the level and type of cognitive challenge, their gender, how the time in lessons is used and the environment the pupils are asked to learn in. When these are all considered, we will begin to teach in a way that works with the brain, rather than against it. As teachers, we all want our pupils to be in a 'place' where they can all learn more efficiently and more effectively in the time we have with them. As such, we need a 'road map' showing the route. What follows in this book are five steps to get there.

Step 1
Learning

What was your favourite lesson at school? What subjects did you find really interesting and look forward to going to? In other lessons did you find it difficult to concentrate despite the best efforts of the teacher?

All the pupils you teach now will also experience this to varying degrees and find your subject and way of teaching difficult, challenging, interesting or motivating. The reason for this is that all our learners possess differences in their psychological and learning 'profiles'. Put simply they are all different and they like to learn in different ways. In light of this, is it appropriate to offer our pupils a 'one size fits all' learning challenge that pays no attention to these differences? The answer is, of course not! What teachers need is an informed understanding and repertoire of ideas to deliver lessons that reflect the broad psychological and learning profiles of all the students we teach, paying particular attention to the variables that most suit how they prefer to learn.

We can begin to develop this understanding by looking at the work of a number of theorists who have developed the notion of the individual nature of all learners. Between them they suggest a range of characteristics that separate learners and learning style preferences. Once we have an understanding of the wide range of learning preferences, we can then build these into how we plan the learning opportunities we give our pupils.

The main theories are the Myers Briggs Type Indicator, Kolb's Learning Style Inventory, the VAK model, the Gregorc model and the Dunn and Dunn Learning Style Inventory.

Myers Briggs Type Indicator

The Myers Briggs Type Indicator (MBTI) evolved from Carl Jung's work on psychological types from the 1920s. It is the most widely used psychological profiling system in business and government today. Though not designed as a learning style detector it is often used for that type of purpose as it includes references to learning preferences as well as other aspects of a learner's personality. If you have an understanding of the variety of psychological profiles of your students, this will then suggest the need for a variety in what and how your pupils are asked to learn. The Indicator uses four pairs of distinctions that can generate up to sixteen individual types.

The four pairs are Introvert/Extrovert, Sensor/Intuitor, Thinker/Feeler and Judger/Perceiver. The analysis produces numerical scores that reveal the extent to which an individual demonstrates these traits. These can range from extreme to mild preference for any of the pairs or somewhere in between.

For the teacher, it is important that learning situations allow all these types of learners to demonstrate their understanding in a way that respects their personality type. As someone can be a combination of personality types, the percentages are for each type and so will not add up to 100.

Introverts

Approximately 25 per cent of the population are reckoned to be Introverts. They prefer tasks that are individualised and prefer working independently. Typically they value aesthetics, are more self-sufficient, more reflective and capable generally of a greater depth of concentration. Activities that encourage art work, writing and individual problem-solving suit this kind of learner.

Extroverts

Around 75 per cent of the population can be described as Extroverts. Typically this kind of learner will welcome variety in learning especially if learning is active and talkative. Interactive, discussion, group work and team activities suit them best.

Sensors

Around 75 per cent of the population are also described as Sensors. This kind of learner relies on external guidance and instructions rather than their own intuition. They are very factual minded and prefer practical applications. They need order and learn best from what is concrete rather than abstract. They prefer activities that produce a definitive answer and conclusion and are more uncomfortable with open-ended tasks and tasks that offer a variety of outcomes.

Intuitors

About 25 per cent of the population can be described as Intuitors. These are life's dreamers. They find theory more interesting than application and are less focused on detail. They like to think in metaphor and fantasy. They are more likely to respond to unconscious processes such as intuition, gut feelings and hunches. They often have a vivid imagination. This kind of learner can handle a lot of complexity within a task and enjoy open-ended instructions that ask for creativity.

Thinkers

Thinkers make up 60 per cent of all males. They are in control of emotions and tend to express them privately. They have difficulty understanding those who are overly emotional. This kind of person is often highly objective and impersonal with a good mechanical aptitude. This kind of learner learns best from listening to the teacher and is more interested in 'what' and 'when' than 'why'.

Feelers

Feelers make up 60 per cent of women. They view Thinkers as cold-hearted and emotionally remote. They see social values as more important than rules. They tend to be much more comfortable talking about and expressing their emotions. This kind of learner is sensitive to the experiences and emotions in others. They work well in learning situations that require empathy, understanding and mutual support.

Judgers

Judgers make up 50 per cent of the population. They typically like to work to deadlines and are very focused on outcomes. They may appear unsettled until a decision has been taken and a problem has come to a satisfactory conclusion. This type of pupil has a highly regulated way of doing things and likes control. They tend to be quicker at decision-making, but dislike situations where they have no plan. This kind of learner enjoys an element of logic in the task, and also tasks that require organising such as sorting and sequencing.

Perceivers

The last category, the Perceiver, makes up 50 per cent of the population. This kind of pupil prefers to keep things open-ended and flexible and is more uncomfortable with closure. They don't work well to deadlines and prefer fun to hard work! They like to take things as they come, have something of a 'butterfly' tendency that means they tend to take on a number of projects at the same time, often without finishing any of them. This kind of learner prefers tasks that require abstract reasoning, multitasking and complexity.

* * *

If you asked your pupils to answer a questionnaire based on this model, it would of course demonstrate that your class is made up of personality types from the full range. Clearly this suggests that learning opportunities within lessons should reflect this range.

Kolb's Learning Style Inventory

Another approach to understanding our preferred learning styles has been offered by Kolb. In the early 1980s, Kolb developed the Learning Style Inventory to evaluate the way people learn. By asking twelve questions the respondent selects one of four possible answers each time. The four possible responses relate to the four ways of learning which are Concrete Experience, Reflective Observation, Abstract Conceptualisation and Active Experimentation.

Concrete Experience

Pupils who prefer to learn through Concrete Experience like active involvement, relating to other people and learning by doing. These learners tend to be open-minded, adaptable and sensitive to the feelings they and others have. The opposite to this type of learner is one who learns through Active Conceptualisation. This is the application of thought and logic to learning. The ability to plan, analyse and develop theories is part of this.

Reflective Observation

Reflective Observation is the characteristic of learners who prefer to watch and listen, take a variety of views and discover meaning in the learning. The opposite to this kind of learner is one who favours Active Experimentation. These kinds of learners prefer to test theories, carry out plans and influence people and events through activity.

Abstract Conceptualisation

This kind of learner enjoys learning about abstract theories and concepts. They are comfortable with not having to have the concrete idea in front of them. They enjoy learning that allows them to plan, hypothesise, analyse and develop theories.

Active Experimentation

This type of learner is best suited to learning that tries out theories and experiments to test them. They have a 'get up and try it' approach to learning. They are the opposite of a learner who enjoys Abstract Conceptualisation.

*   *   *

All pupils at different times will demonstrate the ability to learn in all four of these ways but will undoubtedly prefer one of them. Again, any questionnaire that you might set would reveal a combination of preferred learning styles.

Divergers

You may teach 'Divergers' who are a combination of Reflective Observation and Concrete Experience. This kind of learner can see situations from many perspectives. They do well in idea generating sessions or 'brainstorms'. They tend to be imaginative and emotional and tend to favour art, history and drama.

Convergers

You may have pupils who are the opposite to Divergers and can be described as a 'Converger'. Their results combine Abstract Conceptualisation and Active Experimentation. This kind of learner does well in conventional testing situations or where there is a single correct answer or solution. They can use deductive reasoning and focus on specific problems. They appear unemotional, are better at working with objects than other people and enjoy science.

Assimilators

Results that combine Reflective Observation and Abstract Conceptualisation reveal a learner who is described as an 'Assimilator'. They have a tendency to inductive reasoning and like abstract concepts more than people. They prefer maths and science.

Accommodators

Last, results that combine Concrete Experience with Active Experimentation reveal the 'Accommodator'. This kind of learner likes to be doing things, carrying out plans and performing experiments. They like novel experiences. They rely on others more than themselves for information.

Perceptual Modalities Model (VAK)

Another model for identifying a pupil's preferred way of learning is the Perceptual Modalities Model, or as it is more commonly known, the VAK model. Perceptual Modalities refer to the way we extract data and information from our environment and how these are filtered through our senses. A pupil's dominant modality is the one in which they prefer to 'receive' data or information and is most efficient for that learner. A pupil's secondary preference enhances and clarifies the dominant one.

The three main sensory modalities that are involved in learning are the Visual, Auditory and Kinaesthetic senses, hence the phrase VAK. The ideas behind the VAK model are that teachers should deliver content in a way that suits each of these three senses, therefore suiting a pupil's dominant modality at different times.

The perceptual model offers a rich understanding of how learning occurs. The three modalities each offer a completely different type of learning experience; seeing, listening and doing. It is also possible to divide the three modalities into sub-modalities to increase the range and type of experience in learning.

Visual

This type of learner needs to see the teacher's body language and facial expression to fully understand the content of the lesson. They tend to prefer sitting at the front of the classroom to avoid visual obstructions. They may think in pictures and learn best from visual displays including: diagrams, illustrated textbooks, overhead transparencies, videos, flip charts and handouts. During the lesson, Visual learners often prefer to take detailed notes to absorb the information.

For Visual learners, learning that involves distance, colour, shape, size, sharpness, contrast, movement, proportion and spatial relationships all develop their understanding. Perhaps the modality that has the most potential to develop knowledge and understanding within pupils is the Visual modality. This is because of the brain's design and its natural ability to easily store and process the visual image. In simple terms learning through the Visual modality can overcome learning difficulties that are encountered through an overly semantic approach, as it is the most basic of mental processes. Therefore it offers teachers a far more inclusive strategy to engage and motivate all learners.

Also it has an additional benefit. Research into how to use, and also to retrieve, from our long-term memory suggests that learning through the Visual modality is the key. This is because scan technology, such as MRI and CAT, allows us to see what happens in the brain. There is now strong evidence that neurological processes are directed best via the eyes, such as visual images. Our understanding and insight appears to be heavily dependent on creating images. Stationary images activate the brain and are stored in the long-term memory. The impact on learners of having large images shown to them creates an immediate and lasting impact on the pupil. Large areas of the brain are activated more intensively, the brain cortex is reached more effectively and memory anchors can be created. An image is able to connect parts of already known but disparate bits of knowledge. Visual anchors are created from images on the picture that can be used to retrieve this information later.

The visual dimension to teaching is not only guaranteed to engage the learner but also, if carefully constructed, it can demonstrate, inform and arouse interest. The learner will understand more not only because they are are more fully engaged, but also because subsequent learning will become more simple as these images are easily retrievable from the long-term memory. Pupils will be coming to lessons knowing and understanding more. This is a sure way to improve motivation.

Auditory

For Auditory learners, varying tone, tempo, volume, pitch, timbre and introducing deliberate pauses will all improve their engagement in learning. They tend to learn best through verbal exposition discussions, talking things through and listening to what others have to say. Auditory learners interpret the underlying meanings of speech through listening to tone of voice, pitch, speed and other nuances. Written information may have little meaning until it is heard. These learners often benefit from reading text aloud and using a tape recorder.

Kinaesthetic

Manipulating pressure, temperature, texture, weight and emotional responses will all engage kinaesthetic learners more fully. They tend to learn best through a hands-on approach, actively exploring the physical world around them. They may find it hard to sit still for long periods and may become distracted by their need for activity and exploration.

Gregorc's model

The Gregorc learning model argues that our learning styles are dependent on how we perceive and order information. He argues that our preferred way of learning may be either linear based (sequential) or randomly based (randomized). He also argues that we may prefer to learn in a way that is rooted in the known and observable world (concrete) as well as the world rooted in emotion, feelings and ideas (abstract). So, as we are all capable of being a mixture of these, he arrived at four categories:

> Concrete Sequential
> Concrete Randomised
> Abstract Sequential
> Abstract Randomised

Our learning style would be concrete if we like to learn facts, abstract if we like to learn through making mental pictures to represent a concept or idea, sequential if we like to learn lists and detail in a certain order and, finally, random if we like an idea or fact repeated but without being able to predict when.

Dunn and Dunn Learning Style Inventory

The last learning styles model to be considered is the Dunn and Dunn model. Initially developed in the late 1960s by Dr Rita Dunn, it is now the most widely used learning styles indicator in North America. It is not hard to see why. Of all the models discussed it perhaps offers the most comprehensive overview of a pupil's preferred way of learning.

It is also arguably the most thoroughly researched learning model. It covers the full spectrum of age, ability and gender. But, perhaps most significantly of all, Dunn and Dunn have conducted research to prove that, when teaching and learning through someone's preferred method, attainment actually increases.

Between 1989 and 1990, forty-two different experimental studies were reviewed that used their model. They showed that overall, where students' learning styles had been matched, their results were about three quarters of a standard deviation higher than those students whose learning styles had not been catered for.

Figure 1.1 Dunn and Dunn Learning Style Inventory

This model has its roots in two theories. The first is that an individual processes information differently on the basis of either learned or inherent traits (Cognitive Style Theory) and the second is that the two hemispheres of the brain have different functions so both sides need to be employed during learning (Brain Lateralisation Theory).

Some of the other premises of Dunn and Dunn's model are given below:

- Everyone has different strengths.
- Most individuals can learn if their preferred style is used.
- Differences in preferred learning styles can be measured.
- Attainment rises when teaching is matched to preferred learning style.

The Dunn and Dunn learning style model is based on five categories (see Figure 1.1):

- Environmental (sound, light, temperature, design).
- Emotional (motivation, persistence, conformity, responsibility, structure).
- Sociological (alone, one other, with peers, with adults, varied).
- Physiological (visual, auditory, kinaesthetic, tactile).
- Psychological (global, analytical, right- or left-brain dominant, impulsive or reflective).

The pupil can then find to what extent they are analytical left-brain thinkers who enjoy logic and detail or right-brain holistic thinkers who prefer to see the big picture. Also consider the impact of light and the need for either a well lit space or a darker space with blinds or curtains drawn. Do your students need to stretch and move around perhaps with a snack to maintain concentration or can they sit happily and concentrate for sustained periods of time? Do they prefer a 'hands-on' approach to lessons or do they feel happier listening to lecture-type notes? It will reveal the extent to which your students welcome routine or are happier with change and variety. Finally you will find out if your pupils are self-starters, motivated and persistent or need sustained external pressure.

To establish the kind of learner we are, a questionnaire is answered that produces a score. This will reveal to a lesser or greater extent how pupils are affected by all these variables. Just like any other questionnaire, any class of pupils will reveal a range of learning preferences. The section 'In the classroom' offers an example of the kinds of questions that the Dunn and Dunn model would ask and some guidance on how to interpret the results.

*   *   *

The teacher could be forgiven for feeling slightly overwhelmed by the variety and complexity in understanding how their students prefer to learn. However, three overriding principles emerge from this overview of learning styles.

The first is that there is some duplication across the various models in terms of the characteristics we have in our preferred learning style, e.g. there are Visual learners in the VAK model, the Dunn and Dunn model and the Gregorc model. This means that the range is probably not as daunting as first appears.

The second is that we cannot possibly recognise, process and deliver the different learning preferences our pupils have and teach at the same time. As suggested earlier, all classes will reveal a range of learning preferences across all the models described here. How then, should we begin to address the learning preferences of our pupils given the vast array of types we have discussed? The answer, of course, is that we can't! As teachers the only way we can ensure that we cater for all the many different types of learning preferences is to deliver learning situations that offer an informed diversity. By doing so the teacher will naturally be able to cater for a range of personality types and learning preferences. By constantly varying groupings, type of stimulus and challenge, the teacher will naturally cater for the full range of personality types and learning preferences.

This takes us to the third principle, that variety will also rein-force learning to make it more effective. By delivering content using a rich variety of stimuli such as pictures, discussion, making, doing, saying and hearing, pupils' overall understanding will increase. The following quotes allude to how understanding and learning is improved when more than one way of receiving information is used.

> *We learn:*
> *10 per cent of what we read*
> *20 per cent of what we hear*
> *30 per cent of what we see*
> *50 per cent of what we hear and see*
> *70 per cent of what we say*
> *90 per cent of what we read, hear, see, say and do.*
>   Edgar Dale (Cone of learning)
>
> *I hear and I forget, I see and I remember, I do and I understand.*
>   Confucius (Ancient Chinese philosopher)

The next section entitled 'In the classroom' offers a repertoire of activities to enable teachers to cater for the range of personality types and learning preferences.

IN THE CLASSROOM

If teachers paid heed to every learning theorist, it would soon become very difficult to cater for every learning style and every psychological type. The key however, to address all these different types, is variety. If a teacher delivers sufficient variety then all learning styles and psychological profiles are catered for.

Lesson activities and ideas are offered here for each learning model, demonstrating what should be happening in the classroom.

Box 1.1 Myers Briggs Type Indicator

Introvert

Offer quiet time on individual topics – give an overview of a topic.

Extrovert

Encourage pupils to articulate their understanding verbally. Encourage pupils to explain concepts to each other. Work in groups.

Sensor

Work with facts and raw data. Structure lessons with very clear learning objectives.

Intuitor

Find patterns and relationships among the facts and look for the 'big picture'. Offer a discovery learning approach where the pupils have to understand 'why?'.

Thinker

Set work that involves persuasion and sharing of differences of opinion within groups. They also like precise lesson objectives and dislike vague terms. The more action orientated the better, for example describing what the pupils should do.

Feeler

Pupils like to work in harmonious groups in particular. Work best when everyone has a stake in the group task and everyone sees a benefit for the group. This develops collaborative rather than adversarial working.

Judger

This kind of learner is highly focused on finishing tasks and works very rigidly to deadlines. Use colour-coding e.g. red for vital, blue for background, green for links to previous. Encourage pupils to take a second look.

Perceiver

Pupils like work that involves curiosity and spontaneity. Activities such as 'brainstorming' work to their advantage as well as problem-solving.

Box 1.2 Kolb's Learning Style Inventory

Concrete Experience
Make learning active and learn by doing. Encourage learning that makes the pupils sensitive to the feelings of others.

Reflective Observation
Encourage learning that asks the pupils to watch and listen and to reflect.

Abstract Conceptualisation
Allow learning that plans, analyses and develops theories.

Active Experimentation
Allow learning that develops ideas and tests them.

Divergers
Use lots of discussion and interaction with others. Like activities that require a variety of perspectives so would be good at brainstorming and idea generating. Rely a lot on the teacher motivating them. Show how learning relates to their personal experiences and their interests. Activities that recognise them as individuals suit them too. Like questions that start with 'Why?'.

Convergers
Like to test information, to try things, take things apart and to see how things work and learn by doing. Like things that start with 'How?'.

Assimilators
Good at working with abstract concepts. Like learning to be organised and like to have time for reflection. Work well if given information that is detailed, logical and orderly. Good at gathering a lot of separate pieces of detail and putting them together to form a coherent whole. Prefer to read through a topic alone and resist group work. Like questions that start with 'What?'.

Accommodators
Like learning situations that are highly practical, especially carrying out plans or doing experiments. Experiences that are novel suit them best.

Box 1.3 Preferred Modalities Model (VAK)

Visual

Learn through seeing so tend to see the teacher's body language and facial expression to fully understand the content of the lesson. They tend to prefer sitting at the front of the classroom to avoid visual obstructions. They may think in pictures and learn best from visual displays including: diagrams, illustrated textbooks, overhead transparencies, videos, flip charts and handouts. During the lesson, visual learners often prefer to take detailed notes to absorb the information.

Auditory

Learn through listening so tend to learn best through verbal exposition, discussions, talking things through and listening to what others have to say. Auditory learners interpret the underlying meanings of speech through listening to tone of voice, pitch, speed and other nuances. Written information may have little meaning until it is heard. These learners often benefit from reading text aloud and using a tape recorder.

Kinaesthetic

Learn through moving, making, doing and touching so tend to learn best through a hands-on approach, actively exploring the physical world around them. They may find it hard to sit still for long periods and may become distracted by their need for activity and exploration.

*   *   *

For the following tasks ask your pupils to approach them in the following ways.

Box 1.4 Using the VAK model to teach how to . . .

Task	Visual	Auditory	Kinaesthetic
Spell	Try to see the word.	Sound out the word or use a phonetic approach.	Write the word down and see if it feels right.
Talk	Use words like imagine, picture or see.	Provide listening activities and use words such as hear, tune and think.	Use gesture and expressive movements and use words such as feel, touch and hold.
Concen-trate	Do not distract by movement or untidiness.	Do not distract with inappropriate sounds or noises.	Do not distract with inappropriate movement.
Read	Use descriptive scenes or pauses to imagine the actions.	Use dialogue and conversation and make the characters talk.	Read collabora-tively.
Learn something new	Use posters, diagrams, slides or demonstrations.	Use verbal instructions or talking about it to someone else.	Jump right in and try it.
Put something together	Use directions shown in pictures.	Talk it through with someone else.	Ignore the directions and go through trial and error.

Box 1.5 Dunn and Dunn Learning Style Inventory

Environmental
- Create learning time that involves silent study.
- Create learning situations that have a background sound such as playing Mozart for some extended tasks.
- Ensure learning situations are well lit and bright or work outside on a sunny day!
- Create learning situations with dimly lit rooms, perhaps associated with a mood or theme to learning.
- On cold days ensure that windows are closed and doors shut to keep the place warm.
- On hot days ensure rooms are ventilated. Some students will like to work outdoors when it is cool, others when it is warm.
- Vary the seating arrangements for learning by sitting on chairs, on the floor, on tables, standing or lying.

Emotional
- Set learning goals and challenges to motivate.
- Create a personal meaning to why pupils should learn.
- Reward tasks that are finished to stated deadlines.
- Ensure some learning is multitasked so that there are a number of tasks to complete to finish one overall assignment or project.
- Set very clear guidelines and expectations for some tasks.
- Encourage other pupils to create their own expectations about learning and behaviour.
- Set up some learning tasks where pupils decide the remit and parameters.
- Celebrate pupils who follow class rules – concentrate on applauding the behaviour you want rather than criticising what you don't want.
- For some tasks don't explain the process, but encourage pupils to think of their own.
- For some tasks explain the routines and patterns to what should be learnt.
- Suggest to pupils that for some tasks they should explore a variety of ways of doing them.

Sociological

- Encourage tasks that have to be done alone.
- Encourage tasks that have to be done in a pair.
- Encourage tasks that have to be done in a group.
- Offer the opportunity for pupils to check their learning with you directly if they wish.
- Offer opportunities for pupils to share their learning with another adult in or out of school.

Physiological

- Explain concepts and content orally.
- Create the opportunity for discussion, debate and demonstrating in learning.
- Use word-related learning tasks such as crosswords and word games.
- Encourage pupils to use colour-coding systems, charts, visualisation and pictures in their learning.
- Encourage learning that requires building, construction and making.
- Encourage out-of-doors learning, particularly field visits.
- Encourage pupils to 'feel' and empathise with the learning.
- Allow pupils to sip water during lessons but only at designated times.
- Use morning sessions for learning that requires sustained concentration.
- Use some morning sessions for learning that requires less sustained periods of concentration.
- Use afternoon sessions for learning that requires sustained concentration.
- Use afternoon sessions for learning that requires less sustained periods of concentration.
- Involve movement in some learning situations.
- Ensure that learners have to stay seated in some learning situations.
- Introduce humour and surprise in learning.

Psychological

- Give pupils the 'big picture' first.
- Mix up the sensory input of information through pictures or storytelling.

- Make some learning clearly focused with a specified outcome.
- Give lots of detail to some learning tasks.
- Encourage learning that involves spontaneous responses such as brainstorming.
- Encourage reflection in learning – with questions such as: what was the most important thing you have learnt here and why?

*   *   *

Case study 1.1 centres on a teacher who is trying to offer a range of activities that cater for a broad range of learning styles during lessons in the forthcoming term. He intends to then plan the delivery of the content in response to the kinds of answers he gets from the questionnaire.

Case study 1.1

Dave is looking at the list of pupils that he will be taking when the new term starts in September. He has not taught them before so knows very little about them. He is anxious to get to know something about all of them quite quickly. In particular he would like their views on not only how they like to learn but also the kinds of learning experiences they find difficult or dislike.

He begins to design some questions that the pupils will answer. The questions are designed to reveal the kinds of activities they like to do. Some of the questions ask the pupils to describe these activities without prompting or help.

Dave realises though, that these responses will be dependent on the types of lessons the pupils have so far experienced. Therefore if they have only experienced a narrow range of activities in their lessons, then they won't have much to draw on. So Dave decides to design a part of the questionnaire that offers a 'wish list' of activities that the pupils can select. The idea is that as Dave subsequently planned his lessons, he will structure them so that at some time all the selected activities will be used.

Dave has done some reading about preferred learning styles. This made it clear to him that his class would have, undoubtedly, different preferred modalities for receiving information. He knows his 'wish list' should reflect this range.

This is the questionnaire that Dave came up with:

1   Which are your three favourite subjects or lessons?
2   What kinds of activities do you like to do in these lessons?
3   How do you think that your friends would describe your personality?
4   What are you best at?
5   What kinds of things happen in lessons that you find difficult or boring?
6   Tick each of the boxes for activities that you would like to do in your lessons:

☐   Puppets
☐   Jigsaws
☐   Making models

☐   Making board games
☐   Drawing pictures
☐   Looking at pictures and diagrams rather than doing lots of writing

☐   Talking to a friend about what you have learnt
☐   Working together in group activities (listening to others and sharing ideas)
☐   Talking to the class about what you have learnt by doing presentations

☐   Writing long individual assignments
☐   Project work
☐   Lots of other independent work where you are told what to do and the teacher lets you work alone on it.

Choosing the first three activities suggests that the pupils like doing and making so can be described as Kinaesthetic learners. The second set of three points describe activities that Visual learners would enjoy and the third set of activities appeal to his Auditory learners. Dave anticipated that the first nine activities should be collaborative, encouraging pupils to listen to each other and work together. The three activities at the end were designed to help identify the type of learner who prefers working independently. The results highlighted not only a range, but interestingly that all the pupils chose the puppets activity on their 'wish list'. Dave realised immediately that this looked like a good one to 'hook' the pupils straight away!

*   *   *

Case study 1.2 seeks to address the issue of how to deliver a specific element of content in a way that caters for a range of learning styles. This is a common problem among teachers who are keen to develop the range of learning opportunities, especially for content that is traditionally seen as difficult.

Case study 1.2

The English department are planning how to deliver a forthcoming Shakespearean play that has traditionally been seen as difficult and challenging. Previously the play had been taught with a great deal of teacher input. The majority of lessons had been characterised by the teacher standing at the front while the class listened. The only elements of variety the department had were a video of the play that they showed to support pupils' understanding, and a visit to a local theatre to see the play live. Finally, the pupils were then given a number of assignments that were designed to test their understanding of the play.

Initially the group decided on a wish list of variables that they felt would help the pupils learn the content far more effectively. As well as keeping what they already did, they also came up with:

- Use of classroom peripherals to support the understanding of the play (key characters and their role, key events and key themes).

- Give the pupils a range of ways that they can demonstrate their knowledge and understanding – individual, paired and group work.

- Memorable start or hook to each lesson – suggest finger puppets of main characters, or jigsaw that shows an overview of the play in pictorial form.

- Lots of storyboarding and use of pictures to illustrate content.

- Change the times when the lessons have sustained concentration (sometimes mornings, sometimes afternoons).

- Introduce choice in how the pupils are asked to learn the content of the play through a cartoon strip, an oral presentation, mime, role-play or a combination of all.

- Within the classroom the department were keen to develop a cooperative atmosphere where deadlines were mutually agreed and the process of learning was agreed and shared with the whole class.

- This strategy was agreed and formalised through their departmental planning systems.

*   *   *

Case study 1.3 concentrates on the teacher who feels ready to develop the notion of learning preferences further.

Case study 1.3

Nicki knows the kinds of things her pupils like to do in lessons and the type of activities they dislike. Using this information, she has organised her lesson planning to reflect the ways her pupils like to learn, concentrating on a variety of input suggested by the VAK model. She now wants to take this further and show her pupils how using knowledge about how you prefer to learn can work positively for them, especially when learning out of school. To do this, she suggests to her pupils that they take a copy of a questionnaire that is similar to one Dunn and Dunn compiled when designing their Learning Style Inventory.

Rather than decide herself which pupils should take a copy, she feels that it would be more beneficial if the pupils decided for themselves if they felt ready to use the results. Some pupils needed a little encouragement to take it but no pupil was discouraged. She hoped that this knowledge would help empower the pupils to learn more effectively. The pupils simply tick the statements that they feel very strongly reflect them.

The questions are as follows:

Name _____   Group _____

1 I like to have quiet when I am concentrating and when I study or read I like to get away from noise and distractions.
2 I like to have some kind of background noise such as music or the TV on when I am studying and I find it hard to study when it is absolutely quiet.
3 I prefer to work where there is lots of light and dislike working when the room is dimly lit.

4   I prefer to work where it is dimly lit and like most of the lights off when I study.

5   I like to work when it feels warm and comfortable and can't think when it feels cold.

6   I like to work when I feel cool and dislike it when it gets too warm as I can't concentrate as well.

7   I prefer sitting upright at a desk or table when I study and dislike lying down when working.

8   I prefer to stretch out often on my bed when I study or even read lying on the floor. I dislike sitting at a desk or table.

9   I would describe myself as motivated and want to do really well in school.

10   I would describe myself as fairly disinterested in school and would much rather do other things. No one really cares if I do well.

11   I think teachers would say I am good at getting work in on time.

12   I only get things finished on time when I am interested in them and prefer to have lots of things to do at the same time.

13   I think my teachers would describe me as someone who always has to be reminded to get things done and I often put them off to the last moment.

14   I think my teachers would describe me as someone who always follows the rules and respects authority.

15   I think my teachers would describe me as someone who likes to challenge authority, and I believe there are too many rules.

16   I think it is very important that people accept when they have done something wrong. I try to.

17   I prefer to have fun than serious study and if I make mistakes I rarely admit to them or put them right.

18   I much prefer to have very clear guidelines on how to do things and do better as a result.

19   I much prefer to work things out myself than to do things that I am told.

20   I like routines and when I have them I like to stick to them.

21   I like to find new ways of doing things and enjoy variety.

22   I much prefer to work alone than in a pair or group.

23 I much prefer to work with a classmate or discuss things with one friend.

24 I much prefer to work on projects with three or four friends as this often gives me a better understanding.

25 I like working with groups of students as it makes it easier for me to learn as we help and listen to each other.

26 I don't like to work with people who are in authority or to talk over difficult tasks with someone who is superior.

27 I like to have a teacher or coach to help me understand things that I find difficult.

28 I find it important that my parents are interested in my studies and I like it if another adult member of the family helps me.

29 I remember best when I can hear the lesson and like it when I listen to others teach me and learn best when discussing, listening and explaining to others what I have learnt. I like reading and prefer books.

30 I like to learn when I can see lots of colour, pictures and graphics. I like to visualise things and can often picture what the outcome will be to a problem that I have to solve.

31 I really enjoy learning with my hands and like to work with materials that I can touch and feel. I like to build things. I really like to go on field visits to help me learn.

32 I know I learn better when I feel good about what I have to learn.

33 I learn best if I am allowed to eat or sip water while I learn. I often get a little hungry or thirsty when I work.

34 I don't like to snack or drink when I have to learn as it distracts me. I very rarely think about food or drink when I am studying.

35 The time I find it easiest to concentrate is in the morning.

36 The time I find it easiest to concentrate is around the middle of the day.

37 The time I find it easiest to concentrate is in the late afternoon or evening.

38 I find it hard to sit still for long periods of time and like to get up and stretch or walk.

39 I am quite happy to sit for long periods when I have to study and don't feel the need to move.

40   I like to have an idea about the whole of the learning before I start it and like humour in lessons.

41   I prefer it if there is no humour in lessons and the teacher sticks to what should be learnt in a step-by-step way.

42   I get bored quickly and often don't think before I speak. I often make snap decisions.

43   I like to think carefully and reflect before I answer questions and don't like to be rushed into an answer.

How does the teacher interpret the results?

The questions can be subdivided into five categories. The first eight questions are concerned with the effect the environment can have on how we prefer to learn, in particular sound, light, heat and layout. The results explain the relative impact of each of them.

Questions 9 to 21 are concerned with the issue of emotions and in particular pupil motivation, persistence, conformity, sense of responsibility and need for structure in learning.

The third category, sociological, is addressed through questions 22 to 28, examining the extent to which we like to learn on our own, in pairs, small groups or larger groups and working with adults.

Questions 29 to 31 look at the physiological and in particular the preference for Visual, Auditory or Kinaesthetic learning.

Finally, psychological is the last category and is addressed by the last twelve questions. It examines the extent to which pupils are analytical, global, left or right hemisphere dominant, impulsive or reflective learners.

When the pupils look at all the answers that they have ticked, they could write a profile of themselves (with or without the teacher's help) describing how they like to learn. This should be highly individualised perhaps with a photo of themselves and drawings to represent where, when and how they like to learn.

*   *   *

This chapter has demonstrated that different parts of the brain process different functions. As such we need to offer learning opportunities that utilise the whole brain. The reason for this is because each pupil we teach has a unique learning and psychological profile. To cater for these differences we have to seek to constantly plan a broad variety of activities and learning situations. This range will reach all parts of the brain.

If we do this we will also enjoy the additional benefit of increasing the level of understanding within our pupils. A multisensory approach to learning not only supports individual differences, it raises performance too!

The next section 'Where next?' offers the reader more detailed references to the discussion, ideas and models that have been offered here.

WHERE NEXT?

This section of the chapter will be of interest to teachers who want to further develop their knowledge and understanding of the development in the theory of preferred learning styles.

The Myers Briggs Type Indicator is underpinned by the work of Carl Jung. His contribution to the field of psychology is seen in his work on psychological types. For a useful overview of Jung's work, make a visit to his website (www.cgjungpage.org). Here, under the link to Introduction to Jung, the reader will have access to an excellent overview of his work. His work inspired Isabel Briggs-Myers and Peter Briggs, who both developed the Myers Briggs Type Indicator. A good introductory text to their work can be found in *Gifts Differing: Understanding Personality Type*. For teachers who want to take a detailed test of the Myers Briggs Type Indicator, there is an excellent one online with seventy-two questions available free from (www.humanmetrics.com).

David A. Kolb has his own website that overviews all his work and publications (www.learningfromexperience.com). There is an excellent section on frequently asked questions (FAQs) that the reader may wish to pursue. However the best starting point is probably his book, *Experiential Learning: Experience as the Source of Learning and Development*. This gives much more detail on the development of his four-stage learning cycle.

The VAK model has grown largely out of the work done within the field of Neuro-Linguistic Programming (NLP). A good starting point to study Neuro-Linguistic Programming is *Introducing NLP – Psychological Skills for Understanding and Influencing People*. It develops the idea that all individuals have a preferred modality to receive information. By learning in a way that suits their dominant modality it becomes easier to accelerate the process of modelling excellence, one of the key principles to NLP.

Further reading on the Gregorc model can be found by visiting the website www.gregorc.com. Dr Anthony Gregorc's work on the Mind Styles Model can be more fully explored through the FAQs as well as a comprehensive reference to previous work.

The best starting point for a fuller overview of the work of Dr Rita Dunn and Dr Dunn can be found from their book *Teaching Secondary Students Through Their Preferred Learning Style*. Teachers interested in a more detailed overview of the workings and function of the brain could consult *Discoveries in the Human Brain: Neuroscience Prehistory, Brain Structure and Function* by Louise Marshall.

Step 2

Cognition – intelligence and thinking

THEORETICAL BACKGROUND

Intelligence

How is that some of the weakest pupils are able, in certain situations, to exhibit a level of intelligence and understanding that leaves you surprised? For example, if I asked one of my most 'reluctant learners' how to strip down a motorbike, he would be able to effortlessly describe the process to me. In some cases this would be with a clear and well-thought-out explanation.

Similarly, others would be able to plan a fishing trip that consists of planning transport, an overview of the lakeside location identifying the best position, a prediction of the likely weather as well as an appreciation of the type and weight of tackle to use.

These are the same pupils that in a 'traditional classroom' exhibit all the characteristics of slower learners. They would also score poorly in conventional IQ-type intelligence tests.

But are these pupils intelligent or not? The answer is that it depends on how you view intelligence. There is now a school of thought that suggests that everyone is intelligent but not necessarily in the same way. As teachers we should keep sight of this fact and allow learning to cater for pupils with different intelligences.

Gardner's Multiple Intelligence theory

It was Howard Gardner, a professor at Harvard's Graduate School of Education, who challenged the traditional view of intelligence in the early 1980s. He claimed that intelligence has a unitary capacity that cannot be adequately measured by IQ tests. His theory defines intelligence as an ability to solve problems or create products that are valued in at least one culture. Gardner believes that each person is born with a full range of capacities and aptitudes: though some are naturally stronger and others weaker in each individual. These differences do not mean that one person is any more intelligent but rather they are intelligent in different ways.

Gardner drew upon findings from evolutionary biology, anthropology, developmental and cognitive psychology, neuropsychology and psychometrics to arrive at seven different criteria to judge a person's type of intelligence.

There has been some debate over whether the seven original intelligences are indeed intelligences or whether they are better described as competencies. In any event all teachers would recognise that all their pupils have different strengths. Again, just like the observations from the previous chapter on learning, only an informed diversity of learning situations will benefit the different strengths/competencies/intelligences that your pupils will have.

Below are the different types of intelligence described by Gardner.

Verbal/Linguistic

The Verbal/Linguistic intelligence helps pupils to communicate and make sense of the world through language. One of the most important skills taught in schools is the ability to use language for effective communication and personal growth. The kinds of skills taught are reading, writing, listening and speaking. This intelligence also includes creating stories, using metaphors and similes, symbolism and conceptual patterning. Linguistic intelligence is also demonstrated through the use of humour, jokes, puns, play on words and the ability to quickly acquire other languages.

Musical/Rhythmic

The Musical/Rhythmic intelligence helps pupils to create, communicate and understand meanings made out of sound. One of the ways in which your pupils may exhibit this type of intelligence may be tapping out intricate rhythms on their desk with their pencils. They might like to have soft music in the background to help them concentrate.

Logical/Mathematical

The Logical/Mathematical intelligence helps pupils to appreciate abstract relations, use deductive and inductive reasoning and critical thinking. Pupils with a strong leaning to this intelligence may like to develop strategies, perform experiments, reason things out, work with numbers and explore patterns and relationships. They are typically highly methodical and work well with calculators and computers.

Visual/Spatial

The Visual/Spatial intelligence helps pupils perceive visual or spatial information and to create visual images from memory. They can have acute perception of form, shape, depth, colour and texture. They tend to have active imaginations and are good at expressing their ideas and thoughts through drawings, paintings, sculpture, patterns and colour schemes.

Body/Kinaesthetic

The Body/Kinaesthetic intelligence helps pupils to use all or parts of the body to create or solve problems. This kind of pupil wants to bridge the gap between mind and body. They like to learn through touching, physical movement, manipulating concrete objects, interacting with their environment and 'making and doing'. They also like to stand, stretch and move in the classroom.

Interpersonal

The Interpersonal intelligence helps pupils to make and see distinctions in other people's feelings and intentions. This type of pupil can see situations from various perspectives. They like organising, collaborating, communicating and solving problems between people. They notice and react well to the moods of their friends and classmates.

Intrapersonal

The Intrapersonal intelligence helps pupils to distinguish among their own moods and feelings. This type of pupil is in tune with their own thought processes, attitudes and reactions. They are good at taking responsibility for their own learning. They typically enjoy working alone and are more uncomfortable in groups and will not usually volunteer to make whole class contributions.

*   *   *

The next section 'In the classroom' has an example of a questionnaire that can be done with pupils to help them identify their dominant and weaker intelligences. Since his original seven intelligences, Gardner has gone on to develop his theory of Multiple Intelligences further to include two or possibly three more: Naturalist, Spiritual and Existential. Pupils with a strong Naturalist intelligence will recognise and discriminate among objects found in the natural world. They typically like being outdoors and engaged in anything that has strong links and appreciation of nature such as fishing, hiking or birdwatching. Gardner has rejected the idea of a Spritual intelligence for now as he feels that it doesn't match all the criteria he originally used to determine what constitutes intelligence. He is still deciding whether we have an Existential intelligence. This would be demonstrated through a pupil who is concerned with some fundamental questions about existence. He is still gathering evidence on this one.

* * *

Thinking

Another aspect to developing the cognitive skills of our pupils is to develop their capacity to think! Teachers can very often be heard to bemoan the fact that teaching starts to get more challenging and the pupils more restless when pupils are asked to think! It demands the ability to do several things ranging from being able to describe, comprehend, apply, analyse, synthesise and evaluate.

We need to ensure our lessons challenge pupils and that we have a repertoire of action statements that we can use. We will then know that our pupils are going to be challenged to think!

Bloom's Taxonomy of Thinking Skills

In the 1950s Benjamin Bloom designed a Taxonomy of Thinking Skills to categorise the level of abstraction of questions that are found within educational settings. These Thinking Skills are still the most useful guide for the teachers because they can be ranked from low to middle to high order Thinking Skills. The development of the use of Thinking Skills can be planned by the teacher as the level of questioning can be pitched to the cognitive ability of the pupil.

Box 2.1 Bloom's Taxonomy of Thinking Skills

Type of Thinking Skill	Skills demonstrated and action questions to use
Knowledge	• Observation and recall of information • Knowledge of dates, events, places • Knowledge of major ideas • Knowledge of subject matter *Action questions* *(list, define, tell, describe, identify, show, label, collect, examine, tabulate, quote, name, who, when, where)*
Comprehension	• Understand information • Grasp meaning • Translate knowledge into new context • Interpret facts and compare and contrast • Order, group and infer causes • Predict consequences *Action questions* *(summarise, describe, interpret, contrast, predict, associate, distinguish, estimate, differentiate, discuss, extend)*
Application	• Use information • Use methods, concepts and theories in new situations • Solve problems using required skills or knowledge *Action questions* *(apply, demonstrate, calculate, complete, illustrate, solve, examine, modify, relate, change, classify, experiment, discover)*

Analysis	• See patterns • Organise of parts • Recognise of hidden meanings • Identify of components

Action questions
(analyse, separate, order, explain, connect,
classify, arrange, divide, compare, select,
explain, infer)

Synthesis	• Use old ideas to create new ones • Generalise from given facts • Relate knowledge from several areas • Predict and draw conclusions

Action questions
(combine, integrate, modify, rearrange,
substitute, plan, create, design, invent, ask
'what if?', compose, formulate, prepare,
generalise, rewrite)

Evaluation	• Compare and discriminate between ideas • Assess value of theory and presentations • Make choices based on reasoned argument • Verify value of evidence • Recognise subjectivity

Action questions
(assess, decide, rank, grade, test, measure,
recommend, convince, select, judge, explain,
discriminate, support, conclude, compare,
summarise)

*　*　*

The following section offers over a hundred lesson ideas that utilise
all the different intelligences and thinking skills.

IN THE CLASSROOM

Intelligence

As all pupils have different strengths and weaknesses in terms of their dominant intelligence, teachers need to engage in classroom learning activities that utilise all of them. Again, the key is informed diversity. What follows are over a hundred ideas for lessons that draw from the intelligences described earlier. Keep sampling different activities at different times when planning lessons, so that ultimately, all pupils are taught in their dominant intelligence.

Visual/spatial intelligence

Visual/spatial intelligence relates to visual perception of the environment, the ability to create and manipulate mental images, and the orientation of the body in space. It may be developed through experiences in the graphic and plastic arts, sharpening observation skills,

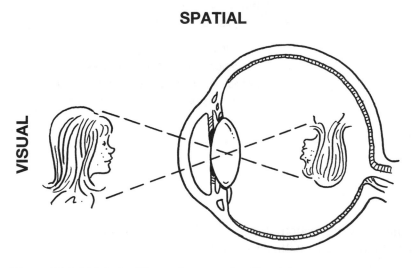

Figure 2.1 Multiple intelligence lessons: visual/spatial

solving mazes and other spatial tasks, exercises in imagery and active imagination. This kind of learner is 'picture' smart. The visual intelligence is most memory friendly.

Multiple intelligence (MI) activities

Draw or paint a picture, poster or sketch – representing what they have learnt without using any words. The pictures should replace words and so be self-explanatory.

'Shoe box' – make a three-dimensional model where references to colour design and scale are needed. Using a shoe box, cut off one long and one short side to reveal the inside. This can then be a place or room that the pupils can use to label, draw and stick items to represent something they have learnt.

Create a colourful design, shape or pattern to illustrate a scene from content learnt in class.

Imagining and visualising how important figures may have changed events using mental pictures. The pupils should close their eyes while the teacher talks to them about a scene/place or event from their learning. The pupils have to visualise the scene as though they were there, using the commentary or visual clues to help.

Taking photographs to create a story or explain a process. Done quickly and easily with a digital camera where mistakes can be rectified with no extra costs. Becomes a good sorting and sequencing activity when the photographs are mixed up and need rearranging.

Construct props and costumes to dramatise an event.

Developing colour-coding systems to categorise information. Encourage careful selection of colours. For example, choose red as an action colour or the colour that goes next to the most important reason. Choose green as a more passive colour or yellow to signify optimism.

Visualisation exercise – by listening to an oral commentary, the pupils visualise the environment as though they were there. Builds empathy skills and increases understanding.

Enhancing line drawings – for pupils who want to draw pictures to represent their understanding but are not confident artists. Create the outline of the picture in dots and the pupils then join them up and embellish the picture with colour and extra detail.

Pictures from memory – see Case study 2.1 (pp. 68–9).

Storyboarding – take any topic that has been learnt and design a cartoon strip that tells the story. Use captions underneath the pictures. These can be done individually and collated to get a group response.

Pictionary – works very well as an overview of a topic. The pupils draw an image to represent the content. The teacher or fellow pupil calls out a fact or statement and the pupil with the correct picture holds up the card.

'Scrap-booking' – involves getting the pupils to collect as many references to a particular topic as they can. Typically this may involve tearing references from old magazines and newspaper supplements as well as cereal boxes or advertising flyers. It could be any concept, place or person. Stick them all onto one sheet of paper as an overview.

Concept maps – can be done either to start a topic or as a review – use a large piece of paper and randomly note all the relevant information in bubbles – the class then agree the relationships between the information and note these by arrows with writing on them that connect all the bubbles.

Memory maps – similar to concept maps but follow the idea that the central idea is noted in the middle of a large piece of paper. Using the metaphor of a tree, from the central concepts the main themes extend out like the main branches, from each main branch sub-sections of information are noted, and then from here, as though the leaves of a tree, are the finer points of detail. Use lots of pictures and colour. Particularly effective as a whole brain learning activity as it uses both left (words and logical sequence) and right (colour, pictures and 'big picture') sides of the cerebral hemispheres.

Visual metaphor – works well for pupils who like to visualise a picture to understand a concept. See example in Case study 2.1 (pp. 68–9).

Wall essays – use large pieces of paper and writing in a size that can be read anywhere in the classroom. Decide on a topic for an extended piece of writing. Divide the content of the writing into several paragraphs. Split class into groups of four and ask each group to write one paragraph to contribute to the overall essay. Each group will have a different paragraph. When this has been finished, stick each paragraph on the wall in random order. This then becomes an active sorting activity as the class decides on the most appropriate order. The correct sequence to the essay should then follow.

Displays as learning tools – high-quality displays that have key learning points and illustrations on them can increase the long-term recall of this information by as much as 70 per cent. The displays have to be legible from anywhere in the room and situated at eye level.

Logical/mathematical intelligence

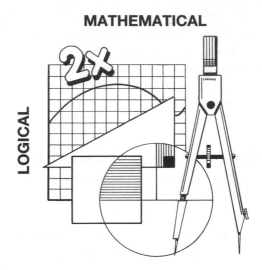

Figure 2.2 Multiple intelligence lessons: logical/mathematical

Logical/mathematical intelligence involves number and computing skills, recognising patterns and relationships, timeliness and order and the ability to solve different kinds of problems through logic. It may be exercised through classifying and sequencing activities, playing number and logic games and solving various kinds of puzzles. This kind of learner is 'number' smart.

MI activities

Create trivia games – these can become quite complex with a number of penalties and bonus points depending on the difficulty of the question. Excellent for a mixed ability class where questions based on simple factual recall score low marks but complex answers requiring a deep understanding score highly.

Developing crosswords and other puzzles for classmates to solve – the crosswords tend to be more difficult but are excellent ways to recap key knowledge. Mix up the crossword so that some of it has the words written in the crossword but with no clues, and the other clues are given but obviously with no words. A simpler but still popular alternative word puzzle is the word search. Mainly effective as a tool to help with spelling.

Constructing a timeline and filling in details – good for history lessons especially, as it encourages pupils to understand negative numbers as they calculate time periods through BC to AD. Useful in English lessons too when, for example, tracing the chronology of a story.

Writing 'how to' books – these allow pupils to demonstrate a high degree of understanding as the 'how to' books should take the reader through a whole process without error.

Problem-solving – any activity that requires pupils to arrive at a solution to a problem. Easiest if the questions start with 'Why?'.

Diagramming procedures – using the same concept as the instructions accompanying flat-pack furniture. There should be no writing, but instead a series of pictures in a step-by-step procedure. The pupil will ultimately have put together something that will help them understand content, e.g. the parts of a section of anatomy.

Create a Venn diagram – to organise information to present to others – works well when separate pieces of information have to be interrogated to find relationships and links. Any number of circles can be used. Overlapping circles mean there are common connections.

Using pattern blocks, unifix cubes, Lego and other maths manipulatives – good to demonstrate concepts, for example in chemistry, to demonstrate compounds, and also good where building something explains how it works.

Categorising facts and information (databases and spreadsheets) – inputting 'raw' data that have no obvious relationship or pattern changes when analysed through a spreadsheet. Pupils can see patterns and trends that can help understanding such as the most common and least common, and timing.

'Diamonds' activities – see Case study 2.1 (pp. 69–71).

Playing cards – design a set of cards that has content on one side. There are many ways to adjust the format, but one approach is for the pupils to hold four or five cards each as in a game of poker. The teacher makes a statement and the pupil who feels they have the best response 'plays' their card. If they are wrong they lose their card, if they are right their card is placed in the middle and they are still in the game. The objective is to be the person who guesses right for all their cards and so wins the game. If there are two people left make the questions harder to create a winner.

Board games – any format will work such as 'Snakes and ladders'. The point is that at some point there have to be question cards or spaces that demand correct knowledge to progress. Games can of course be 'themed' around the content.

Flow diagrams – these can be used for learning that has a beginning and end. Using blocks and arrows to show how one event leads to another. Increase the complexity with extra inputs into the main sequence.

Mysteries – see Case study 2.3 (p. 77).

Linguistic/verbal intelligence

Linguistic/verbal intelligence involves reading, writing, speaking and conversation in one's own or foreign language. It may be exercised through reading interesting books, playing board games or card games, listening to recordings, using various kinds of computer technology and participating in conversation and discussions. This kind of learner is 'word smart'.

Figure 2.3 Multiple intelligence lessons: linguistic/verbal

MI activities

Writing a journal – this can be based on content done in lesson or simply their own reflections.

Create real or imagined correspondence between characters
– good as a way of checking knowledge and understanding.
For example, in a geography lesson it might be letters between an environmentalist and an MP regarding the position of a new road.

Writing scripts that depict events – this can be based on any topic such as the discovery of DNA.

Writing newspapers from a different time – complete with then-current events, fashion, entertainment and features.

Rewrite difficult information in a simpler form – tell the pupils that the work they produce will be sent to the junior schools for the younger children to work from.

Interview a famous person – with prior knowledge of the topic, discussing their accomplishments. In French lessons it might be a cultural icon who is interviewed such as a fashion designer.

Invite a guest speaker to class – this could be a pensioner who is asked to talk about the area or their childhood. Excellent if the pensioner is a relative of one of the pupils as the pride and self-esteem of the pupil rises immeasurably.

Reading poetry/novels/biographies – of people and events related to lesson content.

Designing bulletin boards – the class collect any material that is relevant to the lesson content such as publicity material for films, plays and books as well as any articles or posters.

Using recording devices – dictaphones especially are useful as a way of summarising key learning points. Good fun to play to rest of class.

Doing dramatic readings – creating an element of pathos to reading content raises interest levels especially if the content is particularly important such as a discovery, or the culmination to a plot.

Email important figures – these can be to anyone from MPs, people from sporting/popular culture, academics to interest groups.

Listening to videotapes with no picture – play a section of video but turn the TV around facing away from the pupils. They have to listen carefully to the dialogue and then suggest what the film would have shown. The teacher then replays the video clip and checks.

Discussion circle – sit pupils in a circle and suggest that every pupil has to say at least one thing related to content. Build a whole class response from everyone's input. Good for revision.

Persuasive writing – convince someone of a certain viewpoint based on the power of argument.

Creating a bibliography – the internet becomes very useful for this when typing in a keyword search.

Listening to oral testimonies – listening activity that can be from film or audio clips from the internet.

Design and film a current affairs programme – based on a topical subject.

Research electronic references – such as the main encyclopaedias or through a search engine.

'Chinese whispers' – sit pupils in a circle. The first pupil whispers a short sentence that is based on content. This is then passed on with an added sentence. By the end of the circle (minimum four in a group) the last pupil then summarises what their group said. Mistakes are good because pupils can then suggest what the group were trying to say versus what they finished with.

'Talking frames' – pupils are asked to finish a sentence started by the teacher. The idea is that the pupil's response should be a lot longer than the sentence started by the teacher.

Video without sound – play the video but without the sound. The class then suggests a suitable commentary. The video is then replayed and the pupils check their responses with the tape.

Musical/rhythmic intelligence

Musical/rhythmic intelligence (Figure 2.4) involves understanding and expressing oneself through music and rhythmic movements or dance, or composing, playing or conducting music. It may be exercised through listening to a variety of recordings, engaging in rhythmic games and activities, and singing, dancing or playing various instruments. This kind of learner is 'music' smart.

MI activities

Writing an original song, rap or jingle – good for covering key points of learning.

Playing instruments – especially good to listen to if based on content, e.g. Marseilles or 'Last Post'.

Composing or listening to music that conveys the theme or mood of the lesson – music that is dramatic and based on content is best.

Creating a rhythmic way of remembering information – get pupils to design their own 'rap' music to cover content.

Performing a song to summarise information – pupils choose favourite song and change lyrics for new ones related to content.

Design background music – for example to accompany a narration on tape.

Play Mozart while students engaged in extended written tasks to improve brain state for learning – see Chapter 5 on physical environment.

MUSICAL

RHYTHMIC

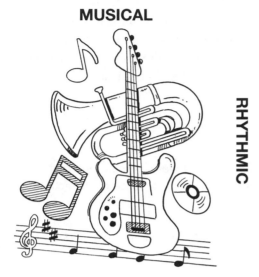

Figure 2.4 Multiple intelligence lessons: musical/rhythmic

Interpersonal intelligence

INTERPERSONAL

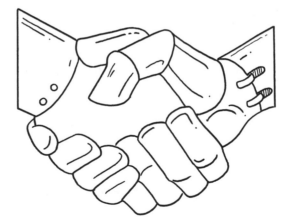

Figure 2.5 Multiple intelligence lessons: interpersonal

Interpersonal intelligence involves understanding how to communicate with and understand other people and how to work collaboratively. It may be exercised through cooperative games, group projects and discussions, multicultural books and materials and dramatic activities and role-playing. This kind of learner is 'people' smart.

MI activities

Working on interactive computer software, email or internet – entering into anything that requires correspondence or interactive responses works well.

Joining any group project – either in class or an interest group outside class.

Identifying with figures – encourage pupils to express the point of view similar to that of a leading character or protagonist from their learning.

Creating imaginary interviews with important figures – similar to above but take this on a step and design questions and likely responses.

Constructing a family tree or 'theory tree' – base it on a character's past or family.

Peer tutoring – teaching anything learnt to younger pupils or parents!

Group presentations to class – discourage an over reliance on reading from a script and dependence on mental notes and short prompts.

Hot seating an important figure – asking questions that need answering from an important personality in their learning. One of the pupils is 'hot seated' – encourage some pupils to pose questions and others to help with answers.

Kinaesthetic/body intelligence

Kinaesthetic/body intelligence involves physical coordination and dexterity, using fine and gross motor skills, and expressing oneself or learning through physical activities. It may be exercised by playing with blocks and other construction materials, dancing, playing various active sports and games, participating in plays or make-believe and using various kinds of manipulatives to solve problems or to learn. This kind of learner is 'body' smart.

Figure 2.6 Multiple intelligence lessons: kinaesthetic/body

MI activities

Dramatise an important event – set the scene in the classroom and act out a scene describing an important piece of learning.

Role-playing – get class to guess what is being described from a role-play situation.

Dance – create a dance or movement that tells a story.

Field trips – a powerful and memorable way of supporting the learning in the classroom.

Learning outdoors – allows for noisy and energetic ways of reinforcing learning such as the action of certain elements in a chemical experiment or quiet, reflective work such as sketching.

Acting out vocabulary words – choose action words from a vocabulary list and decide how to act out for the class to guess.

Constructing projects – making diagrams, models or replicas of systems or procedures.

Making finger puppets – see Case study 1.2 (p. 35).

Shadow puppets – similar to finger puppets but work by joining puppets to a stick and telling a story. Project light behind a white see-through sheet and have the shadow puppets act out a sequence.

Playing charades – excellent way of revising concepts and content.

Handling learning resources – excellent way to bring alive learning resources such as historical artefacts or biology experiments.

Virtual field trips – the internet provides a host of opportunities for virtual 'visits' to help replicate the real thing such as to the Louvre.

Videotape active learning situations – digital technology allows for instant feedback on performance and chance for class evaluation, e.g. set pieces in physical education.

Human timelines – pupils divide themselves up into important events along a time continuum.

Floor maps – use the classroom floor and large sheets of paper and other props to explain the layout of important learning situations such as an electronic circuit.

Sequencing – an excellent sorting activity where pupils have to organise a series of pictures into an appropriate order. Very hands-on and active.

Mime – an excellent quiet activity where, because there is no dialogue, the class very often stay silent as they watch pupils mime a learning situation.

Statues – similar to mime but the students have to get into position to demonstrate a learning situation, stay stationary and encourage the class to guess what it is, e.g. soldiers in the trenches of First World War.

Masks – pupils take on the role of important figures by designing a mask representing that figure that will fit the whole face and then acting out or recounting an important learning situation.

Intrapersonal intelligence

Intrapersonal intelligence involves understanding one's inner world of emotions and thoughts, and growing in the ability to control them and work with them consciously. It may be exercised through participating in independent projects, reading illuminating books, journal writing, imaginative activities and games, and finding quiet places for reflection. This kind of learner is 'self' smart.

INTRAPERSONAL

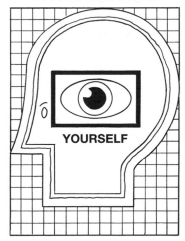

Figure 2.7 Multiple intelligence lessons: intrapersonal

MI activities

Writing journal entries – encourage pupils to summarise content and any personal reactions to it in a journal or learning diary.

Completing independent assignments – excellent for pupils who want to reflect and write up their learning in longer sustained pieces of work.

Mentoring meetings – any opportunity for pupils to discuss their work with a learning mentor such as an older pupil, teacher or other adult.

Investigating complex problems – setting challenging questions that require sustained independent research.

Researching topics of interest – set additional work on a topic that supports and reinforces the main theme.

Creating personal files of topics – personalise the organisation of class work in folders in whatever format the pupil understands best.

Writing first-person accounts of events – write a personal account of an important learning situation as though the pupil is the person such as an inventor, or protagonist or historical figure.

Personalising a character and writing his/her autobiography – choose a figure related to content.

Self-assessing – do projects to determine how to improve learning.

The following case studies (2.1 and 2.2) demonstrate how to use classroom activities that utilise a number of the Multiple Intelligence activities.

Case study 2.1

The history department are keen to develop a range of teaching activities that focuses on the visual/spatial intelligence in particular. From the repertoire of activities listed earlier the history department chooses Diamonds, Pictures from memory, Circles and Finger puppets.

The department realises that the brain is overwhelmingly visual. As such, material that is represented in visual form is often the most accessible and so provides some of the easiest ways to build, understand and apply knowledge. The department wants to deliver lessons that are rigorous, meaningful and engaging.

Example 1: Teaching the English Civil War through 'Pictures from memory'

This activity involves competition, energy, concentration, teamwork and the ability to memorise.

Stage 1: Students divide up into teams of four and give each other a number between 1 and 4. The teacher stands by a desk with Picture 1 (see Figure 2.8) turned over and hidden. The pupils who are assigned number 1 then come out to the desk and are shown the picture for thirty seconds after which it is turned over. The pupils go back to their groups and draw/write as much as they can remember. They are given thirty seconds to do this. After this, pupils assigned number 2 come out and repeat the process. This continues until all pupils have had a go, all contributing to the build up of one image per group of four. Stage 2: Once everyone has had *one* go the groups are given one minute to establish what is missing from their drawing and create a strategy to get all the information accurately represented on their sheets (e.g. thinking how to divide up sections or nominating certain images or words to each member of the group). It might be worth suggesting to the students that whatever they try to remember, it shouldn't be more than five different things (as the brain finds it impossible to memorise more than that many at once!). Stage 3: A repeat of stage 1.

This activity clearly offers a far more inclusive, engaging and active approach to learning and understanding the functions. The team with the most accurate representation of the image clearly wins!

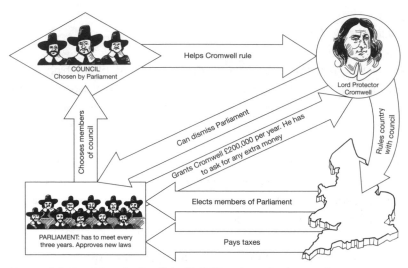

Figure 2.8 Teaching the English Civil War through pictures from memory

Example 2: Teaching the causes of the First World War through 'Diamonds'

This is an opportunity for students to discuss, articulate, debate, ratio-nalise and prioritise nine possible causes of the First World War. The idea is that nine small diamonds are cut out, each with a cause on it. All of

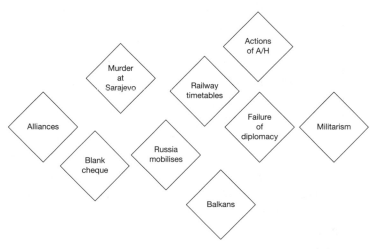

Figure 2.9 Stage 1: the diamonds are emptied from the envelope and placed on the desk (each diamond has a brief title representing a 'cause' of the war)

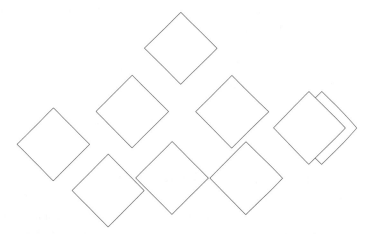

Figure 2.10 Stage 2: the discussions that follow should allow a hierarchy to
         begin to form

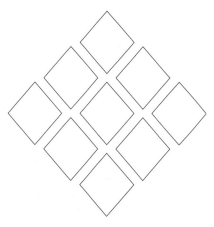

Figure 2.11 Stage 3: a final hierarchy is agreed – hence the term
         'diamonds'!

them then have to be ordered to make the shape of one large diamond,
with the causes of the war ranked from the most important at the top
to the least important at the bottom (1, 2, 3, 2, 1). In practice, almost
without exception the same few causes have found their way to the top
(murder at Sarajevo, alliances, blank cheque) and almost always the
bottom cause has been the railway timetables. This provides the teacher
with a nice little *denouement* to the activity, as the pupils can be reminded

of A.J.P Taylor's view that the whole of the First World War hinged on the railway timetables, as once mobilisation was started it couldn't be stopped!

Figures 2.9, 2.10 and 2.11 demonstrate how the process works:

This activity works equally well for either a cause or effect activity. Similarly, the ranking criteria could be based on short-, medium- and long-term causes rather than importance, or short-, medium- and long-term consequences.

Example 3: Teaching Bismarck's foreign policy through 'Circles'

An excellent visual/spatial activity that can be used either to introduce a topic or as a review at the end of the topic. It also works well as an inductive teaching model.

Stage 1: A large circle is drawn and the students are told that this represents the whole topic or issue, in this case, Bismarck's foreign policy (see Figure 2.12).

Stage 2: More circles are added to the shape and the students are told that the relative size and location of each circle is deliberate and crucial in understanding relationships and relative importance of all the component parts (see Figure 2.13). Why is there a large circle (B) in the middle? This represents the fact there is a large and important element that existed within Bismarck's foreign policy, in this case Germany's relationship with Austria-Hungary. The smaller circle to the right (C) represents how Italy too joined the alliance partners. The large circle (D) that sits outside the main circle represents an influence on the conduct of foreign policy but is not actually part of it. Could this be France? The relatively large size of the circle alludes to its massive influence on Bismarck. France

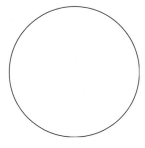

Figure 2.12 A large circle representing the topic

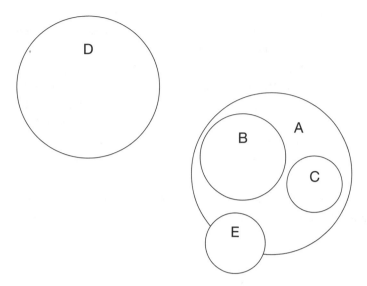

Figure 2.13 Circles showing relationships and importance of component parts

was after all the driving influence behind Bismarckian diplomacy for over twenty years. The circle (E) towards the bottom that is positioned both in and out of the main circle represents a feature that at some time sat within Bismarck's foreign policy but at other times was outside this. Could this be Russia? Initially a Dreikaiserbund partner but eventually allowed to join the entente powers so sitting outside the Bismarckian system. This activity becomes better when it sparks debate over the relative size and location of circles and when students make reference to factors that haven't already been made here, such as the role of Great Britain or the Balkans issue.

What you end up with is a quick, one-stop overview of the topic. Students are very clear about the relative influences, relationships and importance of all the factors that are present when discussing, in this case, Bismarck's foreign policy.

Example 4: Understanding the claimants to the throne of England in 1066 through 'Finger puppets'

The department felt that this could turn out to be one of the lessons that the pupils *will* remember during their entire history course. The reason why this activity extends to something more than a 'gimmick' is because it ensures students take on the role of the principal individuals engulfed in the claims to the throne of England.

Students simply cut out the finger puppets and using the index and forefinger take on the role of each of the main personalities. Using any standard account of the period around 1066, they can bring the characters (see Figure 2.14) forward and then back as their influence ebbs and flows. What you end up with though is a memorable and easily understood account of how each claimant to the throne tried to become king.

The department felt that these activities would be more active and engaging for the pupils and not only were they suited to the visual/spatial intelligence, they were fun too!

Figure 2.14 Finger puppets showing the claimants to the throne of
England

Case study 2.2

Sylvia has just attended a course on Multiple Intelligences and is keen to establish the distribution of the seven original intelligences among her classes. She decides to set a questionnaire. Once pupils have answered each of the questions they then plot them on the chart (see Figure 2.15) that accompanies it.

Rate the following statements on a scale of 1–5. If you score 1 it means that you strongly disagree with the statement. If you score 5 it means that you strongly agree with the statement. If you score 3 it means that you neither strongly agree nor strongly disagree. Once finished plot your results on the chart below.

1	I am skilful in working with objects	
2	I have a good sense of direction	
3	I have a natural ability to sort things out between friends	
4	I can remember the words to music easily	
5	I am able to explain topics that are difficult and make them clear	
6	I always do things one step at a time	
7	I know myself well and understand why I behave as I do	
8	I enjoy community activities and social events	
9	I learn well from talks, lectures and listening from others	
10	When listening to certain pieces of music I experience changes in moods	
11	I enjoy puzzles, crosswords and logical problems	
12	Charts, diagrams and visual displays are important to my learning	
13	I am sensitive to the moods and feelings of those around me	
14	I learn best when I have to get up and do it myself	
15	I need to see something in it for me before I want to learn something	
16	I like privacy and quiet for working and thinking	
17	I can pick out individual instruments in complex musical pieces	
18	I can visualise remembered and constructed scenes easily	
19	I have a well-developed vocabulary and am expressive with it	

20	I enjoy and value taking written notes	
21	I have a good sense of balance and enjoy physical movement	
22	I can discern pattern and relationships between experiences or things	
23	In teams I cooperate and build on the ideas of others	
24	I am observant and often see things others miss	
25	I get restless easily	
26	I enjoy working or learning independently of others	
27	I enjoy making music	
28	I have a facility with numbers and mathematical problems	

Once each of the 28 questions has a score, look at Figure 2.15. You now have to add the scores that correspond to questions 5, 9, 19 and 20. These scores all correlate to the linguistic intelligence. If the

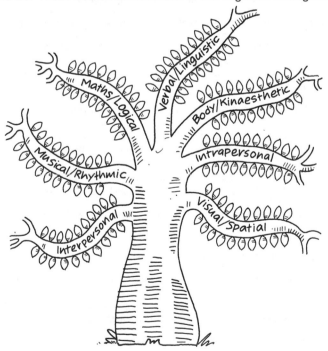

Figure 2.15 Tree of Multiple Intelligence

total score for these four questions is 10, shade 10 leaves on the 'verbal/linguistic' branch, starting at the base of the branch. Do the same for the other six intelligences. The amount of coloured leaves corresponds to the total score.

When she collected the results of all seven intelligences, it demonstrated that there was a huge variety in the dominant one. Figure 2.16 shows the results that Sylvia scored when she did the test herself.

She scored 10 on the four verbal/linguistic questions, 4 on the maths/logical, 18 on the visual/spatial, 10 on intrapersonal, 12 on body/kinaesthetic, 10 on interpersonal and 5 on musical/rhythmic.

She was not surprised at her 'high' visual/spatial score as she feels that pictures and colour are important in her teaching. She was unsurprised at the 'low' maths/logical score as she hates anything to do with numbers!

Figure 2.16 Sylvia's scores on the tree of Multiple Intelligence

Thinking

One of the most effective ways to teach thinking skills to pupils is to deliver them through a work unit. The following case study (2.3) describes how a science department wanted to teach thinking skills through the context of a 'murder mystery'.

Case study 2.3

The science team wanted to deliver a really active, interesting and stimulating module to their 13-year-old science pupils. They decided to present the pupils with a mystery to solve. They were told that one of the more notorious members of staff has been found 'dead' in part of the school. Their task was to present the police with a report that attempted to trace the movements of the teacher prior to their fatality in an effort to come up with an explanation of how the teacher had 'died'.

Part of the investigation involved examining blood samples in the lab to identify proteins and other traces. This was to search for evidence of poisoning. The inside of the teacher's wallet was fingerprinted and the contents displayed on the crime room noticeboard. The pupils looked at the contents (bus ticket, donor card, invitation to party, bank statement and money) with a view to suggesting what they might reveal about the deceased.

The pupils were also given a number of clue cards that offered statements related to the incident. Some were deliberate red herrings such as 'The teacher enjoyed a glass of red wine' and 'The teacher had recently been seen with another woman' and others were close to the truth 'there was a dripping tap that leaked onto the floor'.

The report had to consider and refer to all the clue cards. The report had to recreate the last known movements of the teacher and conclude with a likely cause of death.

All these activities involved the full range of thinking skills:

- Knowledge was identified through describing the scene of crime, labelling the blood found at the scene and the contents of the wallet.

- Comprehension was achieved through summarising what the contents of the wallet revealed and the results from the blood sampling.
- Application was achieved through trying to solve the mystery by suggesting what had caused the 'death' based on the evidence (though this may not be right).
- Analysis was achieved through explaining what had happened in a plausible and coherent way by using all the evidence.
- Synthesis was achieved through asking the pupils to consider all the evidence and identify gaps and alternative theories to explain the 'death'.
- Evaluation was achieved through asking the pupils to convincingly distinguish between the strengths and weaknesses of different bits of evidence and offer a convincing summary based on the value of all the evidence.

*   *   *

The following section 'Where next?' offers more detailed references to the ideas behind Multiple Intelligence theory and thinking skills.

WHERE NEXT?

Intelligence

There are a number of texts that offer a more thorough examination of Howard Gardner's theory of Multiple Intelligence and a more detailed view on the development of these ideas over the last twenty years. Titles such as Gardner's *Frames of Mind: The Theory of Multiple Intelligences*, *Multiple Intelligences: Theory in Practice* and *Intelligence Reframed: Multiple Intelligences for the 21st Century* will all do this.

For a far more detailed reference to how a school may make a structural change to the delivery of the curriculum through MI, Gardner's work on *The Unschooled Mind: How Children Think and How Schools Should Teach* will help. There are a number of more detailed texts that focus solely on Multiple Intelligence activities in the classroom such as *Multiple Intelligence in the Classroom* and *7 Kinds of Smart: Identifying and Developing your Multiple Intelligence* both by Thomas Armstrong.

There are over 600,000 links to the search request 'Multiple Intelligence theory' but a more refined search reveals a number of useful internet links on Multiple Intelligence theory and application in the classroom such as the Disney Learning Partnership site found at www.thirteen.org/edonline/concept2class/month1. This explains among other things, as many other sites do, the theory, relevance for the classroom, criticisms of the theory and the benefits of applying the theory for pupils. There is a useful online test that can be taken to identify your dominant and weaker intelligences demonstrated through a 'snowflake'.

Thinking

Amazingly there are over five and a half million links to the search request 'thinking skills in the classroom'. Many of these sites offer a résumé of what constitutes thinking skills and how to incorporate them into teaching. Some practical support can be found from offering help in creating the thinking classrooms through infusion of thinking skills explicitly so that pupils recognise and utilise thinking skills.

The standards site www.standards.dfes.gov.uk/thinkingskills offers among other things an excellent overview of the history of thinking skills development and a number of case studies. They also link to other useful internet resources such as www.teach-thinking.com and www.sapere.net.

Step 3
Gender

Is there a difference in how boys and girls learn? Is there a need to employ different strategies that respond to the neurological and biological characteristics boys and girls have? Equally, what should we do in the classroom to develop and support the weaknesses that boys and girls have?

Do you recognise the following characteristics, shown in Box 3.1, as broadly accurate?

What are the causes of these apparent differences?

Neurological differences between the sexes

Is has been argued that the brain is shaped in the embryonic stage into either male or female (after about six weeks from conception). The factor that causes this shaping to become either male or female or degrees in between, is the activity of the foetus. The male foetus

Box 3.1 Learning characteristics in boys and girls

Boys

- Boys tend to be more competitive and this can be seen for example when competing to sit in a certain place.

- Written work can often be rushed in an effort to complete tasks quickly.

- They generally seem less inclined to make their work as neat as they can, paying little regard for overall presentation.

- As well as presentation, their work often lacks accuracy with spelling and grammar, and content is adversely affected.

- They tend to be more vociferous as a rule even though what they say may not always be as accurate as it should.

- Aggressive or physical 'horseplay' is often more evident.

- Many boys appear more outgoing and friendly and communicative.

- They tend to be more inclined to 'show off' and take centre stage.

Girls

- Many girls are happy to engage in collaborative work with other boys and girls.

- They often are happy to persevere with tasks that may take some time to complete.

- They generally value taking care with presentation, especially with written work.

- Although not necessarily faultless, they are relatively more accurate with spelling, grammar and content.

- Many are quieter than boys and are happier communicating with a small group of friends.

- Displays of 'horseplay' are rare.

- Appear to be more self-conscious than boys and less inclined to allow themselves to be 'centre of attention'.

produces hormones that organise its neural networks into a male pattern. If these hormones are absent then the brain will become female. There are also degrees in between too, where there can be a male brain inside a female and vice versa. There are also differences in the architecture, interactivity and chemistry of the brain. Male and female brains differ in terms of hemispheric organisation (see Figure 0.3). In general, female brains communicate more effectively across the left and right hemisphere. In female brains the section of brain that connects the two hemispheres (corpus callosum) is thicker with more fibres and denser in female brains than male. It appears to be less susceptible to shrinkage with age too. Also, functional specialisms are more widely spread throughout the brain in females. This has led to the notion that females are better communicators (especially under high levels of stress) and are better at multitasking and engaging in intuitive experiences. Males on the other hand tend to be more specialised.

This is evidenced when we look at language between the sexes. It appears to be a major point of difference. For example, this can be seen when we look at the language development of infants and note that females tend to master language more quickly than boys. Over 99 per cent of girls are able to talk by the age of three and in boys it is usually by the age of four. This mastery of language appears to extend into adulthood: on average women use around 7,000 words a day, whereas men use about 2,000.

These differences are explained because language and spatial abilities are more bilateral in females than in men. Also, the number of neurons per unit volume in the auditory cortex was 11 per cent greater in females than in men in a trial study. Similarly, in the auditory area, women had more neural capacity to manipulate language.

Examples of where males perform more effectively:

- hitting a target with a missile;
- mentally rotating an object;
- listening with only one half of the brain.

Examples of where females perform more effectively:

- fine hand control;
- verbal memory;
- average 20 per cent better peripheral vision;
- listening with both sides of the brain.

The female brain makes the person more sensitive to nuances of expression and gesture and a better judge of character. Females are also more people-orientated than men. Boys appear to perform better on tasks and assessments that are:

- task- and action-based;
- experiential;
- information dense.

Girls appear to perform better on tasks and assessments that are:

- extended;
- open-ended;
- multi-concept;
- reflective;
- text-based;
- interpersonal.

Differences as a result of nurturing

The differences in how boys and girls learn can also be attributed to the type of nurturing they have experienced. This impacts on how they will learn.

For example, research has shown the effects family life has on the development of learning. In early life girls are more often engaged in work that benefits the family such as taking care of younger siblings or making food. Is it surprising then that girls are seen as innately nurturing when it could actually be the result of conditioning? Sometimes it is difficult to separate the effects

Box 3.2 Observable differences in the behaviour of boys and girls

Boys	Girls
• Occupy more play space	• Occupy less play space
• Average thirty-six seconds for goodbye	• Average ninety-three seconds for goodbyes
• Read later	• Read earlier
• Talk later (usually by age of four)	• Talk earlier (99 per cent by three)
• Interact with dialogue later	• Construct dialogues and stories in play
• Identify more with robbers	• Identify more with victims
• Are more competitive in play	• Play less competitive games
• Build high structures in play	• Build low and long structures
• Are indifferent to newcomers unless they are useful	• Greet newcomers
• Prefer objects, blocks and building	• Play with living things or similar toys
• Use dolls as 'dive bombers'	• Use dolls for dialogue and family scenes
• Are better visual/spatial learners	• Are better auditory learners
• Talked 'to' more	• Talked 'with' more
• Better at spatial reasoning	• Better at grammar and vocabulary
• Right hemisphere larger than left	• Left hemisphere is larger than right
• Solve mathematical problems non-verbally	• Solve mathematical problems while talking
• Three times more likely to be dyslexic	• Less likely to be dyslexic or myopic
• Have better general mathematical ability	• Have better general verbal ability
• Enrol in more remedial reading	• Perceive sounds better and sing in tune
• Require more space	• Are slower to anger
• Favour right ear	• Listen with both ears
• Differentiated hemispheres	• Less marked differentiation between hemispheres
• Have shorter attention span	• Have longer attention span
• Corpus callosum shrinks 20 per cent by age of 50	• Corpus callosum doesn't shrink
• High tolerance of pain	• Tolerate long-term pain better
• React to pain slowly	

of culture from the effects of biology to explain gender differences. Some societies have been working hard to address this stereotyping through manipulating the types of play and nurturing both sexes enjoy.

Box 3.2 demonstrates the differences between males and females.

If there are differences in attainment between boys and girls it might be because teachers are not coming to terms with these differences and addressing them effectively so that actual attainment starts to match predicted attainment for boys and girls.

If the boys in your school are underperforming it may be because of the following reasons:

- The lack of flexibility to teach relevant subject material that takes account of local cultural characteristics within schools, particularly for boys.
- Assessment is more sequential. This appears to favour girls more than boys. This is particularly so with the use of assignments rather than solely using terminal exams.
- Teacher attitudes appear to favour girls as they tend to have higher expectations of what can be achieved and militate against boys.
- The 'anti-learning' culture demonstrated by boys is endemic in some schools.
- Although boys generally prefer active learning, they have lower standards of behaviour than girls.
- The process of socialisation is different and begins in early primary education. Here boys have to quickly conform to new behaviours that they find difficult to adapt to. This leads to a decline in self-confidence and self-esteem.

*   *   *

The next section 'In the classroom' shows what kinds of learning opportunities should be provided in lessons so that the natural strengths and weaknesses of boys and girls can be addressed.

IN THE CLASSROOM

If we accept that there are broad differences in how boys and girls learn, even if the causes of these differences are not necessarily proven, we have to yet again address the types of learning activities both sexes engage in. There are two reasons for this. The first is to develop their natural strengths and the second is to support their weaknesses.

Tips for classrooms with girls:

- Encourage healthy competitive learning so that girls will not fall behind.
- Encourage the use of writing journals in maths and science so that they can utilise their natural strengths in verbal/written communication to process maths and science data.
- Give special access to technology and ICT so that they can be seen to use it, understand it and lead with it.
- Train girls in the effects of media imagery and its potential impact on their character development and self-esteem.
- Allow group learning to develop self-confidence.
- Don't let girls be overshadowed and instead allow them to take the role of dominant leaders.

Tips for classrooms with boys:

- Turn boy's energy into positive and productive action.
- Enjoy and steer the natural male energy into academic focus and positive behaviour.
- Utilise storytelling and imaginative work to help the male brain develop its imaginative and verbal skills through story making.
- Create learning opportunities that encourage physical movement.
- Encourage learning opportunities that incorporate conflict resolutions and communication.

Improving attainment of boys and girls

Here are some generic strategies to improve the achievement of boys and girls. It attempts to show how to turn weaknesses into strengths. The activities in the top left box are designed to suit the natural learning styles of boys. Similarly the activities in the top right box are designed to suit girls. The activities in the bottom left box are ones that boys may not necessarily enjoy and may even resist, the same can be said for the activities for girls in the bottom right box. This is where the teacher needs to explain the process and the hoped-for benefits for the pupils.

Box 3.3 Strengths and weaknesses of boys and girls

Boys	Girls
Strengths	**Strengths**
• Set time limits (minimum)	• Set word limits (maximum)
• Set word limits (minimum)	• Set time limits (maximum)
• Make accuracy a competitive issue (league tables)	• Set long tasks (extended writing)
• Encourage role-play	• Encourage collaborative learning
• Make learning competitive	• Reward individual efforts
• Make learning active	• Individualise learning
Weaknesses	**Weaknesses**
• Encourage collaborative learning	• Encourage girls to take centre stage
• Two boys and two girls learning on the same table	• Two boys and two girls take centre stage
• Develop listening skills	• Encourage debate
• Encourage personal studies	• Make learning active and energetic

Box 3.4 offers more detail in how the academic performance of boys can be improved too.

Box 3.4 Improving attainment of boys

Promote active learning

Research and anecdotal evidence from schools suggests that boys enjoy and suit active learning the most as it energises, engages quickly and sustains concentration.

Examples:
- The 'Take 5' approach where pupils list five things that they learnt last lesson and compare the list with the next student.
- Ending the lesson with an activity that sums up a key learning point such as the most important thing learnt that lesson.
- Learning through debates, role-plays and research projects.
- Visual construction of concepts and ideas through memory maps, concept maps and spider diagrams.
- Involving boys in the assessment process.

Develop high-order thinking

There is evidence that boys feel that school is too content driven and that learning lacks relevance to their lives. The development of high-order thinking skills involves the ability to solve problems and make decisions. If learning involves high-order thinking skills then boys are likely to connect with the learning more readily.

Examples:
- Using the Bloom Taxonomy from the previous chapter, target activities that use the high-order activities of synthesis and evaluation.

Create effective learning zones

A learning zone is a notion used to explain how a student is situated within a classroom. A student's learning zone is his/her desk and the three students around him/her. Boys tend to choose learning zones that are comfortable and have some affinity with those around him/her. The teacher needs to manufacture effective learning zones.

Examples of how to create effective learning zones:
- Sit pupils boy/girl/boy/girl. Although this may seem antagonistic and unpopular with the students there are some longitudinal studies that suggest a link between increased attainment and this type of seating.
- Two boys/two girls in groups of four. Perhaps a compromise between the above and unrestricted seating. It is designed for boys and girls to learn from each others' strengths but retain friendship groups and mutual support.

Promoting success

All students enjoy and thrive on success. It is the most motivating outcome a pupil can experience.

Examples of how to build success into class are:
- Break tasks into 'chunks' so that each bit is an opportunity for success. This not only makes the learning appear more manageable but also targets are more achievable. The following 'chunks' offer opportunities for success – starts of lessons, question and answers, smaller sections of activities with clear outcomes, the review of lessons.
- Redefine what success is. Ensure that pupils do not view success as finishing top or getting the best marks. Make success a relative thing rather than an absolute thing. Set personal targets and reward with praise when they are achieved.

Effective feedback

Feedback is especially important to boys. So important is it that it can contribute hugely to whether a pupil becomes success orientated, failure avoidant or failure accepting. The most effective feedback can only occur when very clear expectations have been set, clear marking criteria have been given, there is a greater focus on skills and content than presentation, model examples of good work are given.

Recognising and creating learning windows

Learning windows are situations when pupils are at their most attentive and interested. This may not happen often but when it does it is important that these times are not left to pass but the teacher seizes the opportunity to further develop, expand and deepen the pupils' knowledge and understanding. When these learning windows are exploited it helps develop a culture of achievement and interest. It may be a slow and infrequent start but perseverance will pay dividends.

Developing good relationships

Boys thrive on productive and stimulating relationships with their teachers whether this is implicitly or explicitly demonstrated. They place trust and mutual respect highly in the context of how they learn best. From these strong relationships comes the ability to recognise and learn from mistakes. When pupils do not fear failure, they are more likely to persist in the face of failure and are less likely to engage in self-protective behaviour that is less likely to thwart success.

Developing productive pedagogy

Boys responded best to teaching that:

- viewed all pupils as capable of learning;
- saw themselves as facilitators of learning;
- saw pupils' learning as the teacher's responsibility;
- focused more on skill development;
- worked innovatively with the curriculum to create learning windows;
- offered the opportunity to select their learning pathways in terms of content and style of learning.

Incorporating boys' perspectives

Researchers have agreed that it is critical that the curriculum and pedagogy reflects the needs of boys if it is to engage them more fully. Boys like teachers who:

- listen;
- respect them;
- are relaxed, enjoy the day and can laugh at their own mistakes;
- are flexible, adjusting rules and expectations to meet the needs of individual circumstances;
- explain work carefully and make it interesting;
- do not humiliate them in front of the class;
- show no favouritism;
- give them a chance to make mistakes and learn from them;
- affirm all students.

Reflecting on the nature of your interaction with a mixed gender class is a good way to start the process of changing your teaching and learning style to develop the strengths and weaknesses of boys and girls in your classroom. This can be done through a carefully focused and constructed lesson observation (see Case study 3.1).

Case study 3.1

Debbie is concerned about the relationships she has with the boys in one particularly difficult class. Her mentor suggests a lesson observation. The plan is for the observer to draw a layout of the classroom and mark where the pupils sat by gender only and mark them as B (boy) or G (girl). The classroom layout was then marked with B and G. For the duration of the lesson the observer marked every interaction the teacher had with the pupils with one of three possible notations:

✓   A tick was used every time there was a positive interaction with a pupil such as praise or a smile or a nod of agreement or support.

✗   A cross was noted every time there was a negative interaction with a pupil such as a reprimand or a frown or a gesture of displeasure.

−   A dash was used when there was a neutral interaction that could not be described as positive or negative such as a question like 'Have you completed the homework?'.

At the end of the lesson observation Debbie was asked to draw conclusions from what the ticks, crosses and dashes suggested to her. Some stereotypes emerged with small groups of 'naughty' boys dominating negative interaction. Large clusters of girls who had stayed on task and focused throughout much of the lesson, had little or no interaction with the teacher, either positive, negative or neutral. What this exercise does is point out the range and type of interaction between the teacher and boys and girls. Debbie realised that she had to address the fact that there was so little interaction between her and the motivated girls. Similarly, she decided she wanted to address the level of negative interaction with the boys. From the recommendations she had read about motivating boys, she was particularly keen to introduce more 'positive stroking' to increase self-esteem and then follow this up with very active learning situations recommended in the section on Cognition, in particular the example of 'Maps from Memory'.

* * *

The second case study in this section (3.2) looks at a history department who are keen to begin the challenge of improving the attainment and achievement of boys while at the same time sustaining the high attainment and achievement of the girls.

Case study 3.2

The department have recognised that they have to carry out a number of changes. They have decided to target five strategies in the immediate future, embed these as consistent practice, then look to develop three more in the medium to long term.

They have decided that the areas where boys seem to be struggling are:

- extended listening tasks;
- extended written tasks;
- collaborative learning;
- self-confidence and self-esteem.

Therefore, the department proposed to implement five targets. These were:

- *Shorten listening tasks* and 'chunk down'. Rather than go over the whole of the lesson and what tasks are required, the teachers are going to break the lesson down into four parts or chunks (not necessarily of the same time span). The plan is to divide the lesson content into smaller elements of the whole. This will hopefully reduce the requirement for long periods of listening.

- *Develop a much greater use of using pictures and visual stimuli* to replace long written passages. The department is very excited by this particular development. They want to develop the notion of a twin-track approach to learning the content. Essentially they propose to continue with the long written passages for the girls, as they appear to work well for them. However, the boys are going to be offered a much greater focus on visual and pictorial stimuli with the absence of excessive narrative. Instead, learning and understanding will be developed through the analysis and explanation of pictures. There was the added bonus for the department too. This emphasis on pictures over words would create a 'knock-on' effect in terms of future recall and retention of knowledge from using these pictures. The department recognised the brain's ability to remember pictures better than words. This emphasis on pictures will support the preparation for exams.

- *Rearrange seating to 'boy/boy/girl/girl'* in tables of four. The department resisted the idea of boy/girl/boy/girl seating as they felt that it would create unnecessary conflict and even greater antipathy to learning. Similarly, maintaining the status quo was not working. This rearrangement of seating and the potential benefits for both boys and girls were explained to the pupils. This became a good opportunity for the teacher to share ideas about learning preferences in boys and girls and how both sexes can support each other's weaknesses and develop each other's strengths.

- *Develop a positive atmosphere through language, stroking and disposition* by focusing on motivational and positive interaction. This was done by concentrating on describing behaviours and outcomes that the teacher wants rather than what they don't want. Examples would be 'Thank you to all those of you that are listening' rather than 'I am still waiting for some of you to be quiet'. Both sentences are valid but which one recognises the positive? Similarly, it is better to say 'I am looking forward to seeing your best piece of work on this David' rather than 'I hope this is going to be better than the last piece of work you did'. The old saying 'Five pats for every slap' has some value here because if nothing else it shifts the emphasis from negative to positive. Some teachers even thought of the amount of smiling they did during the lesson. Some decided to put a small classroom peripheral at the back of the room that said 'Smile!' in big yellow letters. This was for the teacher not the pupils!

- *Promote active learning* through a complete overhaul of the schemes of work. Each topic was re-written so that teaching and learning activities involved much more making, doing and movement. Drawing from the repertoire of learning activities in Chapter 2 the department selected a number of activities that involved a high degree of active learning such as making jigsaws based on key themes and overviews, board work that involved pupils coming out to the board and writing/drawing ideas and comments based on group work and discussion circles and role-play.

* * *

The third and last case study (3.3) for this section on gender relates to a scenario where a professional tutor is in discussion with a teacher in their first year of teaching. The newly qualified teacher is becoming increasingly concerned with the level of disaffection and de-motivation from her pupils.

Case study 3.3

Andrea has taught a 'bottom' set of eighteen pupils for three weeks now and she already feels that this is her most challenging group of the week. She is desperately looking for 'answers' to alter the mood and atmosphere of her lessons. She doesn't feel that the situation will get any easier as she has to teach food and textiles. She feels that the boys in the group think it is a 'girls'' subject anyway and this compounds any efforts she may make to engage the boys more fully.

The professional tutor begins the dialogue by first reassuring Andrea that this is not a problem that only she faces. The school has a list of pupils across all year groups that are considered to represent extremely challenging behaviour. In an effort to support the staff in coping with this behaviour the school has a staffed 'time-out' room where staff can send these students when their behaviour becomes too challenging to cope with. The professional tutor begins by observing that of the thirty-seven pupils on this list thirty-one are boys. Of these thirty-one boys, twenty-nine are registered as having considerable learning needs most often related to reading and writing and basic numeracy. He also points out that research has shown that pupils with extreme learning needs are disproportionately visual/kinaesthetic learners. These observations begin the process of diagnosing possible solutions.

Andrea thinks that as she teaches food technology, this does in fact lend itself well to the visual/kinaesthetic learner as the subject has lots of hands-on learning. She feels that at the moment there is an overemphasis on writing especially when the pupils have to research a menu, ingredients, process and how they might evaluate it. Andrea wants to shift the emphasis on to the practical and away from the theory. This is especially important as the boys find the written work relatively difficult and so find the learning demotivating.

From the discussions Andrea plans to do the following for an upcoming topic on making a cake:

- Start with making the cake with ingredients and a process that she has already decided on. This will get the boys actively engaged straight away. It will also take the initial emphasis on writing away.

- Encourage boy-friendly designs for the cake such as a snooker table, football field or car shape.
- Develop some sense of connection by suggesting the cake could be for a male relative such as dad, grandparent, younger/older brother or cousin, and that the cake could be given as a present to them.
- Agree to take photos of the cakes at the end to promote self-esteem.
- Agree to take photos if the cakes go wrong as long as there is an explanation of why it went wrong. This will encourage the boys to think that learning from mistakes is not a bad thing.
- Concentrate on discussion rather than writing as a way of evaluating the process, deciding on design and any research. Film this onto a camcorder and encourage the boys to evaluate as a group.

*   *   *

The theoretical background has suggested that in general terms there appears to be an issue within language development between boys and girls. This difference will often manifest itself in a disproportionate number of boys with language-/literacy-related learning needs. This then brings us to the problem of how we can specifically engage and support learners who find the conceptual demands of learning difficult because, initially at least, they cannot access the written material. Moreover, they then find it hard to demonstrate this understanding through a written response. This inevitably leads to a downward cycle of disaffection and demotivation. How can we begin to address this?

Differentiation

Differentiation is simply the planned intervention by the teacher within the learning process. The teacher modifies learning so that the learning needs of all pupils are catered for. There are a number of ways to differentiate. Each approach is, of course, suitable for boys and girls.

Task – This involves designing a number of learning tasks that are suitable for different abilities. For weaker pupils this may involve tasks that require a low cognitive challenge initially. Using the checklist from the section on 'Thinking' from Chapter 2, it may be appropriate to ask questions that demand students to *list*, *define*, *tell*, *describe*, *identify*, *show*, *label*, *collect*, *examine*, *tabulate*, *quote*, *name*, *say who*, *say when* and *say where*.

It is important though, that if these initial sets of tasks are successfully completed, an increase in the cognitive demands of subsequent tasks is made. Again the taxonomy of thinking skills suggests some from the area of comprehension, to application, to analysis, to synthesis and, ultimately, to evaluation. By focusing in this way, the teacher looks on all learners as having learning needs and therefore doesn't focus too much on learning that has a low cognitive challenge.

Support – This strategy revolves around the level of individual support the teacher chooses to give a pupil. Ordinarily it may be that the teacher supports the learner by asking additional questions around the central question to help arrive at the correct answer. However, other adults and other pupils can all become classroom support to various pupils at various times.

Outcome – In some instances it is entirely appropriate to set one task that all the pupils are asked to complete. The way in which this task then becomes differentiated is through the way it is assessed. Put simply every pupil can respond correctly to the task but there will be a variety of responses, with some better than others. The teacher will identify a variety of possible responses from the simplest to the most detailed and complex. Examples of this type of activity involve 'open' questions, the best of which begin with 'Why?'. The responses will be distinguished from simplistic and brief responses that would be assessed at a low level moving ultimately to responses that are detailed, complex and confidently evaluated. Other valid 'open' exercises involve description activities.

Resource – Using a variety of resources with varying complexities would be the obvious way of differentiating by resource. Often the complexity of the text would be a guide to the appropriateness of the material. Short word sentences with a relatively low number of syllables in each word would support the weaker readers while resources with complex and difficult language may be appropriate for the more able pupils.

Pace – Simply encouraging pupils to work more quickly on certain tasks might be an appropriate way of differentiating. This approach may increase understanding and skill development. Working at a slower pace may be an appropriate way of supporting slower learners.

Another approach to differentiation involves dividing the lesson objectives into three:

- all
- some
- few

Or it is sometimes described as:

- must
- should
- could

The teacher decides the basic learning objectives that 'all' the pupils 'must' have learnt. By their nature these should be foundation/ fundamental objectives that are accessible to all the class.

The teacher then has to develop further what are the other suitable learning objectives that 'some' of the pupils 'should' learn. Again, as these are not appropriate for all pupils they are likely to be slightly more challenging. Finally, the teacher has to decide on some learning objectives that only a 'few' of the pupils 'could' learn.

In general terms the low-ability pupils are disproportionately visual/kinaesthetic learners so it is often inappropriate to offer too much written text. Where possible, learning is more effective if it can be delivered through pictures and diagrams with only short written sentences. Similarly, a high dependence on oracy allows pupils to express their understanding without having to feel restricted by their relatively poor literacy skills. Learning by doing rather than writing also allows low-ability learners to access knowledge and understanding.

For very high-ability pupils who generally have a much higher understanding of written material it is more appropriate to challenge them in a predominantly text-based way. There are a number of ways of doing this including:

- work that encourages pupils to learn from a variety of perspectives;
- interrogating a variety of sources of information from a variety of media;
- evaluating information and forming considered judgements;
- sustained independent research.

This approach tends to favour girls more than boys as it requires independent, protracted study with a high degree of text-based work. However, high-ability boys will still find it challenging too (see Case study 3.4).

Case study 3.4

Richard has been teaching a geography group that has eight of that year group's most able pupils. He feels that he is not offering the level of challenge to these pupils that he should. Having considered a number of approaches he decides to plan the following unit of work.

The unit of work focuses on the tourism industry and in particular judging the impact of the tourist industry as either a positive or negative influence within a region.

To develop the complexity, the group of eight pupils is asked to carry out a mini enquiry into tourism within a region of Great Britain (The Lake District) and another region in a less economically developed country (Mediterranean coast of Croatia). The group of eight have to identify the positive and negative effects of tourism on both regions and identify if these effects vary depending on how economically advanced the region is. The findings are then tabulated and discussed within the group.

Once the problems have been identified the group then has to identify solutions. They could imagine they are environmentalists and produce a report that recommends how to maximise the potential benefits of tourism while at the same time ensuring the negative effects are minimised.

This investigation is then broadened to become a national policy for tourism. They have to decide what kinds of questions they might ask and what evidence they might use. A clear understanding of the relative merits of quantitative and qualitative data is needed too.

This report should be a word-processed formal report that might be designed for an international agency or charity.

Finally, the group should conclude with a section on 'recommendations for action' and include a method to effect sustainable economic development. Alternatively, the group may make a recommendation either for or against tourism based on their findings.

*   *   *

This section has demonstrated once again the need for an informed diversity in learning for boys and girls of all ability levels. There are some trends and generalisations that can be made about how boys and girls learn best and also how to best match the learning task to the ability level of all the pupils that you teach. There is an emerging pattern developing where the same learning task may, indeed, be the ideal choice for a certain preferred learning style, dominant intelligence, gender and ability level. As such, the detailed repertoire of learning activities suggested in Chapter 2 allows the teacher to cater for all of the needs some of the time.

To promote effective learning even more, we not only have to pay attention to the preferred way of learning, dominant intelligence, gender and ability but also to how we use the time we have with pupils. Put simply, we can maximise the efficiency of how we use our time with pupils by planning more appropriately. Then we can once again increase the effectiveness of learning. Chapter 4 illustrates how.

WHERE NEXT?

There are a number of texts that further develop the difference between the genders and the effects of this on learning.

Doreen Kimura's book *Sex and Cognition* provides an overview of what is known about the neural and hormonal bases of sex differences in cognitive ability. She demonstrates how there are gender differences in how common problems are solved and these are a result of the effects of sex hormones on brain organisation early in life. She also explains what is not yet known!

Moir and Jessel's book *Brain Sex* demonstrates how difference between gender is also a result of the work of hormones at a very early stage in the life of the foetus. The development of male and female brings distinctive strengths and aptitudes in one that is not shared to the same degree between the sexes.

The idea that the male and female brains are different and have distinctive strengths and weaknesses is further explored in Simon Baron-Cohen's work *The Essential Difference: The Truth about the*

Male and Female Brain. He makes some assertions about what the male and female brains are best suited to doing and draws on a wide range of evidence.

Finally, the book *Sex on the Brain* by Deborah Blum covers a wide range of evidence to explain the characteristics of the male and female, ranging from aggression, nurturing, behaviour, infidelity and homosexuality.

For information related to gender issues in general, the DfES standards site (www.standards.dfes.gov.uk/genderachievement) has a dedicated gender link. It offers an online resource offering help to raise the performance and aspirations of underachieving boys and girls by providing examples of best practice and guidance. Follow the link at the top to case studies and research. There are downloads available offering key findings, for example, in strategies to raise boys' achievement. Similarly, there are case studies from both the secondary and primary sectors.

Step 4

The whole lesson

THEORETICAL BACKGROUND

Many teachers only teach their pupils for a relatively short period of time. In some cases this might be as little as one hour per week. Therefore, teachers would probably like to cover more content in greater detail in the relatively short time they have with their pupils. Is there anything teachers can do to increase the efficiency of learning in this time? In short, can they get more out of the pupils and be able to give the pupils more? The answer is yes. The following suggests ways that the teacher can increase:

- the amount of detail the class covers;
- the amount of detail the class can recall lesson on lesson;
- the level of attention throughout the lesson and aim to keep it high.

This chapter will focus on achieving these aims through the following:

- Improving the quality of the starts of lessons.
- Improving the quality of the ends of lessons.
- Improving the attention rates within the middle of lessons.
- Increasing the quantity of learning through speed-reading and speed-writing techniques.
- Utilising a range of memory strategies to improve recall of knowledge lesson on lesson.

When these are achieved and are coupled with the earlier strategies from the previous chapters that cater for preferred ways of learning, the dominant intelligence, ability level, gender friendliness, you will have a powerful recipe to significantly improve the quality of learning.

Improving the quality of the start of lessons

Figure 4.1 demonstrates that at the start of lessons attention and engagement are at their highest. Also described as the 'primacy' effect, it suggests to teachers that as this is the optimum time to engage pupils, teachers should ensure that it is a time that is focused on high-quality learning. Too often, unfortunately, this time is given over to administrative tasks and organisational issues. Isn't it better to do these slightly later in the lesson and use the start for learning? High-quality starts also ensure that the pupils are tasked straight away so helping with management of discipline. This time also allows pupils to learn something straight away so improving self-confidence and self-esteem for the rest of the lesson. Finally, a well-planned start to a lesson that has the 'wow' factor too, will leave a lasting impression that will engage and motivate learners. The section 'In the classroom' will offer a number of activities that can be used to achieve this.

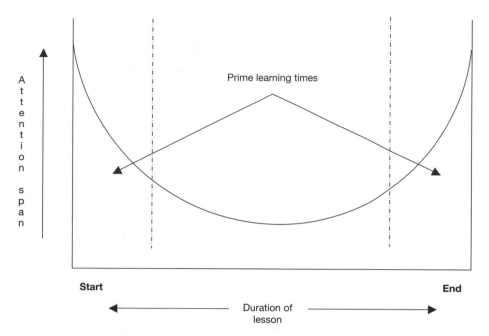

Figure 4.1 Attention rates in lesson

Improving the level of attention during the middle of the lesson

As the brain's natural cycle of attention drops during the middle part of the lesson the teacher has to intervene to bring the level up. What are the best ways of doing this? Using the repertoire of lesson ideas shown in Chapter 2, this part of the lesson is best suited to active, movement-orientated learning activities. If these are introduced, it is very difficult for the pupils' attention to become disassociated with the lesson. If the learning is sufficiently engaging, then the attention span will naturally rise. Lesson ideas taken from virtually all the seven intelligences are best suited here as long as they demand some kind of physical movement. Mostly though these will be found from the kinaesthetic intelligence.

Improving the quality of the end of lessons

Figure 4.1 also shows that at the end of the lesson attention and engagement begins to rise again. The natural attention span of the brain dips in the middle and picks up towards the end. Again, an often quoted criticism of many lesson observations is that at the end of lessons, pupils' learning is not brought together to reinforce and ensure all learning points have been understood. As pupils typically forget around 80 per cent of what has been learnt in a lesson within 24 hours, it is critical that lessons end with a review of what has been learnt. Research has proved that as the frequency of review increases lesson on lesson, there is a corresponding increase in knowledge. Again, the section 'In the classroom' will offer strategies to improve the quality of the end of lessons.

Increasing the quantity of learning through speed-reading and speed-writing techniques

Speed-reading

How can the teacher increase the pace at which pupils are able to read and absorb key concepts and content? What will help the teacher cover more content in a shorter period of time? Teaching some speed-reading techniques will help, but this will only really help those pupils who have a confident grasp of reading already. However, once mastered through repeated practice, the student will be able to cover more in the same time.

The starting position is important. You should sit up straight, hold the information down with your left hand, and use your right hand to do the pacing (the opposite if left-handed). Before you start speed-reading, you should scan the information first to get a general idea of what you will be covering and of the style and difficulty of the writing. These methods are simple to learn but will not do you any good unless they are practised. It usually takes about three or four sessions before you get accustomed to a particular technique. Attempt all five strategies as you may find that one is more suitable for you than the others. Find the one that works for you and use it.

The 'hand'

The first method is to simply place your right hand at the top of the page in the middle. Slowly move it straight down the page, drawing your eyes down as you read. Keep an even, slow motion, as if your right hand has its own mind. Your eyes may not be exactly where your hand is, but this simple motion will help you go faster. Make sure you don't stop until you reach the bottom. Keep the movement slow and easy. Only do it once per page. If you are left-handed use your left hand as the dominant pacing hand.

The 'card'

The next technique is to use a card or a folded-up piece of paper *above* the line of print to block the words after you read them. Draw it down the page slowly and evenly and try to read the passage before you cover the words up. This helps break you of the habit of reading and reading a passage over and over again. It makes you pay more attention the first time. Be sure to push the card down faster than you think you can go. Slide the card down once per page.

The 'sweep'

Another method is to use your hand to help draw your eyes across the page. Cup your right hand slightly. Keep your fingers together. With a very light and smooth motion, sweep your fingers from left to right, underlining the line with the tip of your tallest finger from about an inch from either side of the paper on each line. Use your whole arm to move, balancing on your arm muscle.

The 'hop'

Similar to the 'sweep' method is the 'hop', but in the 'hop' you actually lift your fingers and make two even bounces on each line. Each time you bounce, you are making a fixation that hopefully catches sets of three or four words. Moving to a 'hop' method also makes it easier to keep a steady pace as it is a lot like tapping your fingers on a desk. Balance on your arm muscle, don't just wiggle your wrist.

The 'zig-zag' or 'loop'

The last method is a type of modified scanning technique. Take your hand and cut across the text diagonally about three lines and then slide back to the next line. The idea here is not necessarily to see each word, but to scan the entire area, letting your mind pick out the main ideas. It is a fast way to help you get the general ideas from a body of text.

*   *   *

Speed-writing

Can you read the following sentence?

> Spd wrtng cn be lrnt in abt fteen mints. Jst lve out mst r all vwls
>
> (Speed-writing can be learnt in about fifteen minutes. Just leave out most or all vowels.)

This is one method to develop pupils' ability to take notes more quickly in the time they have in lessons. This may be appropriate in learning situations where a pupil is tasked with collating the ideas of a group quickly or reporting an event watched on video. There are many commercially produced schemes to develop a short-hand style and method. These are often intended for the busy executive who has to digest wordy manuals and reports.

However, schools may find they already have a shorthand method in place! Increasingly teenagers are becoming well versed in the new phenomenon within language communication – the text message. Here, abbreviated words are readily understood by the recipient and sender. If ever there was a ready-made model to support speed-writing, then this is it.

Can you read this sentence?

i hpe tht u av lots ideas 2 tk away w u fm ths bk

(I hope that you have lots of ideas to take away with you from this book.)

Memory strategies

There are a number of stages in understanding how memory works. When you are watching something like a play or film, the brain processes the information it receives from it. The images seen enter the eyes as light waves, what is heard enters as sound waves. In order for you to make use of these waves, this information goes through the following three stages:

1   Encoding – Information is changed and then encoded so that we can make sense of it, such as light waves into images and sound waves into words and words into meanings.
2   Storage – The encoded information is then stored. Memory for a word will include what it sounds like, looks like and what it means. Different types of information are stored in different ways. How we store it affects how we retrieve it.
3   Retrieval – Recovering information from storage is called retrieval.

Improving retrieval of memorised information

Information is better remembered if it organised in a logical or structured way. By organising information you have to think about it. This additional processing helps retain the information and organising it helps make links between parts of the material. The following example of 'memory maps' is a good example.

Research has shown that we remember information better if we also form an image of it. Indeed, the brain has an almost limitless capacity to store visual information. There are tests that demonstrate this to be true. For example, tests done with control groups and 10,000 pictures showed a 90 per cent accuracy in recall up to three months after seeing the picture once. This shows that once the brain sees a picture it is very hard to forget it. Hence the phrase, 'I never forget a face'.

Here are some examples of the use of imagery to help recall information:

1   Method of Loci – Uses a familiar place or route as a link with a list of things to be recalled. For example, imagine having to remember a shopping list. You have to imagine your route to the shops and create an image of each item you have on your list. Try to use the item you want with a distinguishing feature on the route to match the first letter of the item on your list. This will provide an additional aid to recall. For example, imagine a loaf of bread walking into the bank, tomatoes on the traffic lights or biscuits on the building site. This organises memory into a sequence.

  Additionally, a random sequence of numbers can be remembered this way through the Method of Loci. Simply substitute the number you need to remember with a visual representation told through a story or journey. This is one of the ways professional memory experts are able to recall an apparently meaningless sequence of random digits.

2   Linking an image with a word – when, for example, learning a new language, the pupil creates an image that sounds like the new word to be learnt.

For example, five is 'cinq' (pronounced sank) so a picture showing what appears to be a sinking hand emerging from some water would trigger the word sank and so recall 'cinq'. Wine is 'vin' (pronounced van) so a picture of a van with the word wine on the side would trigger the word van and so recall 'vin'.

* * *

The key to effective memory is something that has always challenged humankind throughout the ages. Even from the time of the Ancient Greeks, attempts were made to design a foolproof method for retrieving factual information from the memory. The phrase mnemonics is used to describe any device that is used to help remember something, such as a rhyme. The word is derived from the Greek word 'mnemon' meaning mindful.

For long-term memory retrieval another good method is to think in the following way. The three keys to effective long-term memory recall are:

1 Visualisation
2 Association
3 Location

These are the three principles on which memory champions work. Basically whatever it is they wish to memorise is turned into pictures (Visualisation) that have an association with something specific (Association) and these images are then put into a sequence of a story or located in a place (Location).

These principles can be explained through the following two examples:

1 Learning a sequence of random digits
2 Memorising the correct sequence of a shuffled deck of cards

The way to memorise a random set of digits is to change the digits 1–9 into shapes or objects that are most easily associated with that number. Figure 4.2 gives an idea. You don't have to use these examples if you think of a shape or object you think is more naturally associated with a particular number.

1 =   Candle

2 =   Swan

3 =   Macdonald's sign

4 =   Small sailing boat

5 =   Hook

6 =   Golf club

7 =   Flag

8 =   'Fat lady'

9 =   Balloon on a stick

Figure 4.2 Number associations

So, if the random sequence of numbers was 2, 7, 3, 8, 8, 1, 9, 4, 5 you would have to construct a story where the numbers are transferred into the objects shown in the chart above. They then have to be woven into a story where they appear in the order they fall.

Therefore imagine seeing a swan (number 2) walking grace-fully towards an imaginary golf course and onto one of the greens. In the middle of this golf green is the hole with a flag placed in it (number 7). The swan sticks its beak into the hole and pulls out a ball that has a very distinctive logo printed on it. It's the logo of the MacDonald's hamburger chain, with its distinctive yellow and red writing (number 3). The swan puts this golf ball into its beak and sets off looking for the owner of the ball. As it walks off the green it notices two very large old ladies (number 8 and number 8) sitting on a bench. The two old ladies are looking at the swan. . . .

Your imaginary story would continue until you had used up all the numbers in the order you had to remember them. If you remember the story and the images that go with each number, you will easily remember the correct sequence of numbers. This is the process that memory champions use when memorising thousands of digits. They might have several separate stories though.

The same principles of Visualisation, Association and Location apply when memorising the sequence of cards from a randomly shuffled deck. This time a code has to be developed where every card (apart from the royal and ace cards of each suit) are changed to become two letters. The way to do this is to first change the numbers of each card as follows: 2 = B; 3 = C; 4 = D; 5 = E; 6 = F; 7 = G; 8 = H; 9 = I. So, whatever number card it is, the number is changed to become one of the letters shown previously. Second, the first letter from the suit of that card becomes the second of the two letters that each card will have.

These examples show what happens: The 3 of Hearts becomes the initials CH, the 7 of Clubs GC and the 5 of Diamonds ED. The first letter is taken from the code above and the second letter is simply the first letter from the suit of the card to be remembered.

Now each set of two letters has to become the initials of someone relevant to you. They can be famous or not. So in the example above someone with the initials CH should come to mind. When you have put that person in mind you have to locate them in a place. As the deck of cards unfolds and each card is turned into a set of two initials, simply think of the appropriate person and locate them into your sequence. Good examples of remembering where you can locate them, is to 'put them' in a distinctive place along an easily remembered journey such as a drive home from work, or perhaps along a favourite route for a walk.

If you can remember the faces of the people and their initials in the correct order along a journey or route, you can remember the sequence of the cards. For the royal and ace cards from each suit you can still use the system just described or you might have a direct person come to mind. For example the Queen of Hearts may be Princess Diana and the King of Clubs a successful football manager. When asking pupils to learn and memorise important facts and ideas, simply ensure that the facts are turned into visual images; there should be a strong association between the fact and the image. Then the images should be located in an imaginary story. Remember the story and the facts will take care of themselves.

*   *   *

The next section 'In the classroom' offers some ideas on how you may use the strategies here for improving the efficiency of how the lesson is used. This is so that the pupils can learn more and remember more in the limited time you have with them.

IN THE CLASSROOM

Improving the quality of the start and end of lessons

There are a number of ways to improve the quality of the start and end of lessons. Short, discrete activities that typically last about ten minutes offer a way to begin learning that helps the teacher to:

- Ensure pupils learn something straight away.
- Give the pupils a task straight away so ensuring they are learning at the optimum time.
- Support classroom management by concentrating on working rather than settling the class to listen.

Examples of activities should utilise the three senses of Visual, Auditory and Kinaesthetic. Similarly, a high-quality end to a lesson is vital for effective and long-lasting memory of the lesson's key learning goals. Effective ends to lessons are also sometimes described as plenaries or reviews. The most effective ones are those that:

- Are usually about ten minutes long.
- Focus on learning goals.
- Are dominated by pupil involvement rather than the pupils listening to the teacher simply restating the learning goals without checking the extent to which learning has been successful.
- Are focused on a variety of senses (Visual, Auditory and Kinaesthetic).

Remember that the activities shown in the examples for starters can also be used as examples of activities that can be used at the end of lessons. They are interchangeable. Box 4.1 (p. 116) shows some examples.

Case study 4.1

The English department are keen to develop more effective starts to lessons. They decide to design a sequence of six activities that are focused on the Shakespearean play, *Romeo and Juliet*. They are all designed to be discrete ten-minute activities and are deliberately multi-sensory. Each should reinforce knowledge that should be learnt in that lesson. The expectation is that these activities will be used flexibly so that they can become a template for other lesson starters. These are the suggested activities:

- Lesson 1 – Play a three- to four-minute section of videotape from one of the scenes from the play. Turn the TV away from the class and to the wall. This will suit auditory and visual learners. The class has to *listen* to the video and visualise how the scene unfolds. The teacher stops the tape, rewinds and takes feedback

Box 4.1   Ideas for starters/plenaries

Visual

- Analyse a photograph/painting asking questions such as describe why has this photo been taken or painted, what is the message in this?

- Anagram of an important concept word for that lesson.

- 'Odd one out' – four statements about the lesson, one of which might be false – check at end.

- Word search.

- Crossword.

- Video clip without sound – play a clip of video that has the sound turned off – ask the pupils to write their own description of what is going on.

Auditory

- Audio clip listening to speech or song or oral testimony related to content – teacher reads sample from, for example, speech/play/poem/song or letter.

- Video clip without picture – play a clip from a video with key learning material on but turn the TV around so that the class can only hear rather than see the clip.

- Pupils sit in a circle and tell each other one thing they learnt last lesson and then pass it on.

Kinaesthetic

- Interrogate an object/model or artefact related to a topic being studied. Ask questions such as: What is it? What might it be used for? What does it tell us?

- Model of historical building.

- Role-play a learning situation that might be used for that lesson.

- Demonstrate a structure or concept with the use of props or pupils in an imaginative way.

from the class on what the video was showing. This lasts for two to three minutes. The class then have the video replayed to them with the screen of the TV visible. They compare their predictions to what is actually shown.

- Lesson 2 – Affix either a still from the video or a commercially produced poster connected to *Romeo and Juliet* to the white board. Pose some questions with arrows such as: Who is shown here? What is happening here? Where is this taking place? What comes next? What happened before? A visual stimulus such as this is very accessible for all pupils, allowing all of them to contribute.

- Lesson 3 – Give the class a number of pieces of card, each one showing a scene from the play. They have five minutes to discuss the correct sequence that the cards should go in to follow the plot of the play. The teacher then checks the accuracy. Pupils are asked to consider other possible sequences and how these might affect the course of the play.

- Lesson 4 – The teacher writes four statements on the board. The class have to decide which one is the 'odd one out'. The attraction of this exercise is that there may be more than one possible answer depending on the criteria the pupils choose to use. For example, three out of the four may belong to one family from the play, so leaving one odd one out. On the other hand, however, a different one may be the only one that dies in the play so having a different 'odd one out'.

- Lesson 5 – Arrange the chairs from the classroom in a circle. The teacher explains that the class is going to review its knowledge of the play up to now. The idea is that each pupil makes one contribution to what they can remember about the play and then this is passed along. This is a cumulative exercise whereby the pupil at the end of the circle has to absorb all the ideas the class has. This also works with a number of smaller circles within the same class. To make it a more inclusive exercise, ensure that the weaker learners start the activity and the stronger learners finish it.

- Lesson 6 – A short visualisation exercise can be a powerful way to engage the pupils in the play. Ask them to close their eyes and then read them a short piece from the play. The idea is that you have to engage as many senses as possible, asking them to think carefully about what they can see, hear, touch, smell and feel. This is a good way to try to immerse the pupils in the play and the characters.

The department agreed that these ideas would be easily transferable to other content across other year groups.

Creating 'wow' starts to lessons

It is true that most teachers' repertoires cannot stretch to very many 'wow' starts to a lesson. However, the following five points are elements found in what could be described as a 'wow' start:

1 Complete and utter surprise
2 Noisy
3 Startling
4 Un-orthodox
5 Compelling visual imagery

An example of how complete and utter surprise could be achieved is taken from a history lesson. At the beginning of the lesson, one of the pupils is asked to come to the front. Unknown to the pupil, the teacher has hidden a gas mask taken from the Second World War, together with a card that has instructions on how to wear it correctly. All of a sudden the teacher thrusts the surprise gas mask into the hands of the pupil and shouts 'Gas! Gas! Gas!' in a loud voice. The pupil is then given the card and told to put the mask on correctly in thirty seconds to avoid gas inhalation. The class watch the pupil fumble and panic in their haste to get the mask on correctly. At the end of the exercise the pupil is told that this is the same scenario a young person of their age would have encountered the first time they had put on a gas mask during the Blitz in the Second World War.

A noisy start can be achieved through the careful selection of an auditory piece that has to be dramatic, sudden and likely to go to extremes of sound and tone. It has to be a surprise and elicit fairly strong responses from the pupils creating a mood of 'What was that?'.

A startling beginning to the lesson could be related to an object or item. It should elicit responses that range from the 'urghh!' to the 'wowww!'. A text message from a major celebrity would last long in the memory, as would a particularly stomach-turning biology experiment!

For an unorthodox lesson start imagine the class sitting waiting for the teacher to start the lesson when the teacher suddenly starts to juggle, or stand on the table, or do a handstand or lie on a table. It will certainly surprise the pupils and leave a lasting impression! An unorthodox action is even more powerful when linked closely to a learning point.

Use compelling visual imagery for a memorable lesson start. For example, a picture accompanied by the question 'What is it?' where the answer is far from obvious is likely to encourage much debate and the answer when found will last long in the memory. Unusual design solutions to things such as chairs or tables are good. Also pictures of ordinary objects taken from unusual angles and distances work well here.

Improving the level of attention during the middle of the lesson

Any activity during the middle part of the lesson that requires listening or seeing allows pupils, potentially, to disengage with the learning and effectively 'switch off'. This is the part of the lesson where levels of concentration are at their lowest, so what can the teacher do? The best solution is to focus on learning activities that demand some kind of physical response from the pupil. It then becomes impossible for the pupil to disengage. This might be getting out of their seat, making or creating something that involves physical movement with their hands or body. In Chapter 2 many lesson ideas were offered through the kinaesthetic intelligence. Use this as a checklist when considering what activities to do to raise the attention levels.

Memory strategies

Designing activities that are suited to promoting effective memorising of key learning points is something that would benefit all teachers. There are a number of strategies that improve long-term retention of knowledge, not least the 'Visualisation, Association and Location' method to learn the sequence of the nine planets of the solar system described in the section 'Theoretical background'. Another effective strategy is one that has variously been described as a memory map or brain map (see Figure 4.3). In short, it is essentially a form of note-taking that utilises both the right and left hemispheres of the brain. The idea is that the central theme or topic is noted in the centre of the page. Next draw a number of major themes/ideas stemming from the central topic. These branch out organically from the centre. Each branch has the idea written on it. Stemming from these are smaller 'branches' with subsidiary information on them. Up to this point these maps are based on words and logical sequence (left brain). For them to become a whole brain learning tool, the words should be colourful (right brain) and the map should revolve around the 'big picture' (right brain). For the map to become even more efficient, illustrations (right brain) should be drawn to represent the ideas written. These maps should be highly individual and idiosyncratic making them personal and meaningful to the pupil. Some of the benefits of memory maps are that they:

- give you an overview of a large subject/area;
- enable you to plan routes/make choices and let you know where you are going and where you have been;

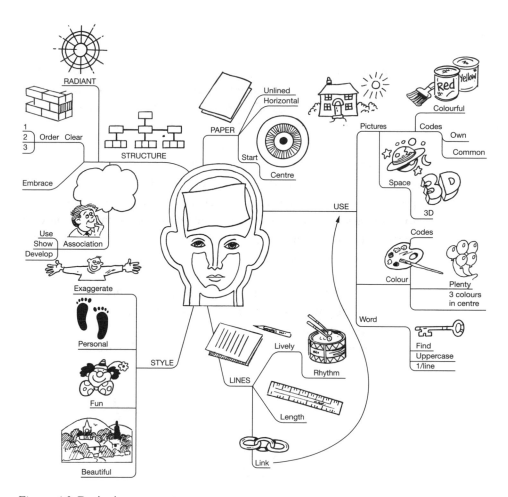

Figure 4.3 Designing a memory map

- gather and hold large amounts of data for you;
- encourage problem-solving by showing you new creative pathways;
- enable you to be extremely efficient;
- are enjoyable to look at, read, muse over and remember;
- attract and hold your eye/brain;
- let you see the whole picture *and* the details at the same time.

*   *   *

Another key to remembering content more efficiently is to examine the importance of the visual intelligence and, in particular, how to utilise pictures instead of words to convey and remember key learning points. The section 'Theoretical background' has shown how the brain's capacity to store visual images is almost limitless. Images are rarely if ever forgotten and they are stored in the brain's long-term memory. Here are some ways to support the use of pictures as a learning tool. Look at the following pictures and try to suggest what they show. They are for a social studies topic on the League of Nations in the 1920s. These pictures are concerned with the following questions:

- What were the aims of the League? (Figure 4.4)
- What powers did the League have to make countries accept its decisions? (Figure 4.5)
- Why wasn't the League very strong? (Figure 4.6)

Figure 4.4 Using images to learn the aims of the League

An interpretation is offered after each picture to demonstrate how the pupils can learn the content without actually reading!

Figure 4.4 shows three things. One is a picture of the world with people holding hands around it. This is meant to represent the idea of collective security. One shows a dove of peace. This should represent the idea of peace. One represents money and the world. This should suggest the connection between money and the world. Therefore, the answer to the first question is that the League had three aims, which were to promote world peace, collective security for the world and to increase the financial state of everyone in the world.

Figure 4.5 represents the three sanctions that the League had. One shows a 'wagging' finger suggesting some kind of admonishment or telling-off. One shows a barrel of oil with a large cross through it and the last shows some tanks. These pictures should suggest that the League had three possible powers to force its decisions to be accepted. The first is to admonish an offending country and ask them to stop. The second is to prevent oil or other commodities going to them (sanctions) and the last power is to use tanks or, more generally, military force. Therefore, the answer to the question about what powers the League had to force countries to accept its decisions would be that initially it could verbally admonish them, it could then decide to stop trading with them or, finally, it could use military force.

Figure 4.5 What powers did the League have to make countries accept its decisions?

 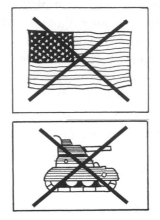 

Figure 4.6 Why wasn't the League very strong?

Finally, Figure 4.6 shows several reasons why the League was unsuccessful in its attempts to become an international force. There is a section that has the flags of Great Britain and France together with two angry and unhappy looking faces looking in. The next picture has another flag, this time of the United States, with a cross through it. A third picture has the same tank as used in Figure 4.5, but this time with a cross through it and, finally, there is a picture of a ballot box with a snail underneath it. These illustrations should suggest that there were a number of reasons for the failure of the League. These include the fact that the relationship between Britain and France did not appear to be a productive one. The cross through the flag of the United States alludes to the fact that the US was not part of the League. The snail next to the ballot box should suggest that voting was very slow, making decisive action difficult. Finally, the same tank shown earlier but this time with a cross through it should suggest that even though the League could have used military action, it never did, thus contributing to its overall failure.

This is an excellent activity that can be done either as a review or revision activity at the end of any topic or it can be used to begin a topic when the pupils have no prior knowledge. Done in this way it can offer a context for the pupils as they move through the content in more detail, aiding overall understanding. Similarly, pupils will become more adept at thinking of helpful pictures to associate with concepts the more they do it. For those pupils who do not feel confident in their artistic talents, the internet provides a rich source of images to use. Simply use the 'image' search function together with a carefully worded search request and many possible images will be available. This is also the most efficient way of doing it, as less time is wasted on colouring and drawing.

*　*　*

The section, 'Where next?' offers some more detail, in particular on research linked to improving long-term memory. It also offers more suggestions about beginnings and ends to lessons as well.

WHERE NEXT?

There is much more detail on the DfES link on using effective starter activities in lessons. By simply following the links through any of the subjects (English, maths, science, ICT and TLF – foundation subjects) there are case studies of good practice to be found. Here you will have an opportunity to see more examples of starter activities to do in lessons. Perhaps one of the best books to use to improve your memory is Kenneth Higbee's *Your Memory – How it Works and How to Improve it*. Here he offers a much greater insight into effective memory strategies such as linking, story systems, and some of the fallacies and truths of mnemonics. He also discusses avoiding interference when memorising and talks about how important it is, when memorising different things, to do so in different locations. Failing this there are again over a million links to the search request 'improving memory' and a good starting point here would be www.mindtools.com which offers a range of different strategies depending on what is intended to be learnt.

Similarly, the internet provides literally millions of links for the search request 'speed-reading' and 'speed-writing'. Though many of these are focused on the commercial market, in particular for hard-pressed executives who need to go through weighty reports but are 'time poor', they do offer transferable skills for the teacher to use. A good starting point would be to follow the link to www. selfgrowth.com/reading/html. This one offers a list of other related websites.

Step 5

Physical environment

Being based in one teaching area or room is not a luxury every teacher enjoys. However, for those who can, they should realise that there is huge potential to maximise learning in their classroom by managing the learning environment productively. Your classroom is, after all, a 'home from home'. Much of your working life is going to be dedicated to this space. You have a high degree of control over the quality of the physical environment you choose to work in.

As suggested earlier in the Introduction, the classroom should become the teacher's silent helper, assisting in creating the right conditions and environment for effective learning. The environment is second only to the teacher as the most important factor in pupil success in learning. The idea that the environment is a factor in intellectual development has stemmed from research on the way the brain changes in response to certain external stimuli. This research has a long history.

Research background

The idea that changes in the brain morphology can occur as a result of external influences has been evident from as early as 1815 when a scientist called Spurzheim reported that the brain, as well as other muscles, could increase with exercise as these areas have more blood carried to them as they are 'excited'. Even Charles Darwin mentioned that the brains of domestic rabbits were smaller than wild rabbits. He thought this was because domestic rabbits did not have to exert their intellect, instincts and senses as much as wild rabbits.

It wasn't until the 1960s that more work was done on the effects of enriched environments on the brain. This work demonstrated that enriching the environmental condition in which rats were confined could alter both the chemistry and anatomy of the neo-cortex and, in turn, improve the animals' memory and learning ability.

In 1997 at the Salk Institute of Neuroscience in the US, researchers found that rats who were exposed to an 'enriched environment' grew 15 per cent more neurons in the hippocampus. These enriched environments were designed to stimulate the senses of the rats through visual, intellectual and physical stimuli. Although much of the work has been done on rats, there are other studies of the effects of an enriched environment on the nerve cells and their neurotransmitters in the cerebral cortex on several mammalians such as monkeys and cats as well as some bird species.

Similarly, there are isolated studies on humans too. Using a number of deceased individuals, studies were carried out that examined the portion of the cerebral cortex that is responsible for word understanding, the Wernicke's area. This examination showed that those deceased who had been college educated had more dendrites in their nerve cells than those deceased who had only had a high-school education.

There has, however, been some over-interpretation of this work. This work does not show that an enriched environment *improves* the visual/spatial memory but rather that if *deprived* of this kind of environment it has been proved that the brain suffers. The message for our classrooms is clear. Make them as multi-sensory and stimulating as possible. Depressing and poorly kept learning spaces actually inhibit effective learning. Therefore, we should acknowledge that there is no such thing as a neutral learning space.

What kind of physical learning environment should we aspire to? Should it:

- be stimulating to look at?
- be practical and flexible to work and to learn in?
- provide stimulation to learners and teacher?
- offer motivational stimuli?
- be a place learners and teacher can feel proud of?
- have controlled and appropriate levels of lighting, temperature and sound?

Making the visual environment stimulating

One of the surest ways to motivate pupils and promote self-esteem among them is through displaying their work on high-quality display boards around the classroom. However, while this is a powerful incentive to display, more room should also be made for using display as a learning tool in the classroom. This can still celebrate pupils' work but it can also assist the teacher. There are real benefits to doing this. By using displays that are legible from anywhere in the room and positioned at eye level, long-term recall of these learning points can be as high as 75 per cent. If the teacher replaces these learning displays frequently, then obviously more knowledge can be learnt, almost passively, in this way.

What is a good test of judging the impact of display used as a learning tool? If you take the time to put up a new display, watch the response from a class when they enter the room for the first time. It will certainly attract their gaze and then after a while, once the display has been changed, ask them to reflect on what was there previously. They will have remembered most of it whether they wanted to or not!

The most effective displays are not necessarily two-dimensional either. Particularly for pupils who are in education from eleven, it is perhaps rare for them to see classrooms that have three-dimensional displays. These can be highly attractive and effective. Take for example the English teacher that has been doing some work on the 'horror' genre. One corner of the classroom has essays on the horror genre that model good practice. However, hanging from the ceiling using very thin wire are some characters such as Dracula and Frankenstein, drawn, coloured and cut out and extending to about three feet in length. An impressive backdrop! Other opportunities to improve the quality of the visual environment might be to paint and colour-code tired old cupboards, storage areas or lockers.

Any work that is displayed should also be motivational and aspirational. If it is used as a model of good practice some helpful arrows and pointers identified on the work will show other pupils why the work is good. The teacher may also decide to display classroom peripherals that are focused on motivation and are success-orientated. These may be quotes (some famous, others made up) designed to improve self-esteem and to encourage the pupils to reflect and strive for personal improvement. For example, posters that read:

'Smile at least seven times in this lesson'

'You are now entering the "Academy for Learning" – please enjoy!'

'This lesson is the beginning of the rest of your life – make the most of it!'

Inspirational quotes might be:

'The future belongs to those who believe in the beauty of their dreams'

Eleanor Roosevelt

'If you can dream it, you can do it'

Walt Disney

'Always remember that your own resolution to succeed is more important than anything else'

Abraham Lincoln

'Be not afraid of growing slowly, be afraid only of standing still'

Chinese proverb

Layout

There are a number of powerful arguments for a change in arrangement of seating and tables. First, different learning activities (mentioned in Chapter 2) need different seating arrangements. In a typical classroom with fifteen tables and thirty chairs there are many, many different ways of organising these to suit different learning situations and circumstances. The other compelling reason for periodic change in seating and table arrangements is that the brain remembers particularly effectively when the learning situation is novel. Therefore, if a new topic is to be introduced together with a host of key learning points, it makes sense for the teacher to lay the classroom out in a novel way as the brain will naturally associate the novelty of what has been learnt in that lesson with the novelty of that layout. The section 'In the classroom' offers a number of ways of arranging seating to fit a variety of purposes.

Colour

Perhaps as teachers we do not give much attention to the issue and potential impact of colour in our classrooms. However, as any colour therapist would tell you, managing the colour environment can have significant benefits for all of us, not just our pupils. These benefits range from physical and mental to emotional and spiritual. The idea is that the seven colours of the spectrum can balance and enhance the body's energy centres or 'chakras'. Studies have been done with various groups of people, plants and animals that demonstrate the effects of different colours on emotions and behaviour as well as growth. This has been utilised by hospitals, prisons, industry and commerce. By learning how colour influences us, we can effectively use it as an extra boost of energy when we need it. Colour therapists would contend that the seven colours of the spectrum have the following characteristics:

Red – vitality, courage and self-confidence
Red is the kind of colour that helps create energy. Motivational posters are best typed in bold red letters.

Orange – happiness, confidence and resourcefulness
Orange is the best emotional stimulant and strengthens our appetite for life. Greetings and smile posters are best typed in orange.

Yellow – wisdom, clarity and self-esteem
Yellow is related to the ability to perceive and understand. Problem-solving activities could be best typed in yellow.

Green – balance, love and self-control
Green helps relax muscles, nerves and thoughts. It helps create a mood of renewal peace and harmony. Green is a good colour to use if you have a space dedicated to quiet work and introspection.

Blue – knowledge, health and decisiveness
Blue is a mentally relaxing colour that has a pacifying effect on the nervous system and aids relaxation. This colour is ideal for worksheets. As it helps calm hyperactive children, it is also an excellent choice for the colour of classroom walls.

Indigo – imagination, dreaming and intuition
Indigo connects with the unconscious self and strengthens intuition, imagination and dreaming activities. Posters that are aspirational and goal-setting are best typed in this colour.

Violet – beauty, creativity and inspiration
Violet purifies our thoughts and feelings and gives us inspiration and enhances artistic talent and creativity.

The implication of this knowledge for the classroom teacher is that careful thought should be given to the choice of colour to suit a variety of circumstances ranging from walls and display space to worksheets and letters. All have a potential impact and choosing more wisely could start to support our work in the classroom.

Smell

Similar to the observations made about colour, the teacher should be aware that the careful manipulation of smell can also have possible benefits for learning The most relevant point is that there is a very strong connection between smell and memory. Aroma processing is wired directly to the Limbic system (see Introduction p. 1) where memory is stored. Early anatomists called this part of the brain the 'smell brain' and believed it was primarily olfactory in nature. Smells may trigger a memory, either recent or distant. Therefore, it is sensible to introduce a distinctive smell while perhaps revising a certain topic or key piece of learning. Revisiting the smell later should trigger recall of that learning.

Certain smells can be helpful in enhancing relaxation. One famous study was done where patients had MRI scans. When the vanilla-like aroma of heliotrope was introduced, 63 per cent of patients showed reduced anxiety. In Japan, the Shimizu construction company utilises the air-conditioning system to release certain aromas in order to improve alertness and concentration, alleviate stress and to relax workers. They also demonstrated how keyboard errors were reduced with the aid of lemon scent.

The implication for teachers is that if we introduce fragrances that relax or refresh our pupils, this can have a beneficial impact on ensuring we improve the overall quality of learning. See Box 5.1 for some examples of smells and their benefits.

Box 5.1 Scents and their purposes

Scent	Purpose
Lemon, peppermint, lily of the valley, floral scents, lavender, jasmine, mint, eucalyptus	To reduce errors and increase work rate
Spiced apple, rose, chamomile	To reduce stress
Vanilla, neroli, lavender	To reduce anxiety
Basil, cinnamon, citrus flowers	To relax
Peppermint, thyme, rosemary	To energise
Woody scents, cedar, cypress	To relieve tiredness

Music

Recently educators have been extolling the potential benefits of music in promoting effective learning. Indeed, some studies are suggesting that musical training can boost non-musical intellectual skills. Such is the enthusiasm for this that, in 1998, the governor of the state of Florida in the US agreed that the state would pay for CD recordings of classical music to be given free to new mothers as they left hospital.

A lot of this recent enthusiasm can be bound up in the phrase 'the Mozart effect'. This term was coined by Alfred Tomatis for the alleged increase in brain development that occurs in children under the age of three when they listen to the music of Mozart. The idea for 'the Mozart effect' originated in 1993 at the University of California with physicist Gordon Shaw and Francis Rauscher, a former concert cellist and an expert on cognitive development. They studied the effects on eighty-four college students who listened to the first ten minutes of the Mozart 'Sonata for Two Pianos in

D Major'. They found a temporary enhancement of spatial–temporal reasoning as measured by the Stanford–Binet IQ test. This is the ability to form mental images from physical objects or to see patterns in space and time. These skills are critical for example, to work in engineering and architecture in understanding proportion, as well as in geometry and other mathematical and scientific concepts.

The same team then tested the idea several years later on seventy-eight much younger children. They were split into four groups. One group received piano lessons, another singing lessons, another computer lessons and then the last group received no extra lessons. By the end of the research they were able to show that the pupils who took extra piano lessons had improved their scores by 34 per cent for an activity that asked them to piece together a puzzle of a camel. The effects of the piano music this time seemed to last longer so leading to speculation that sustained music-focused study could lead to a lasting change in the brain.

There has also been some work done on the effects of different types of music on rats. Essentially the research found that the rats that had been exposed to classical music were able to run through a maze more quickly, making fewer mistakes, than the rats who had been exposed to other stimuli.

Perhaps the most impressive benefits to listening to music and practising music can be found in maths. For example, research done in the US using the music of Hungarian composer Zoltan Kodaly, found that pupils who had received musical training in his specialism (singing songs that are sequenced in difficulty), raced ahead of their fellow pupils in maths.

Some other claims have been made about the benefits of listening to certain types of music. Recently, a book called *The Mozart Effect* has condensed the world's research on this. Some of the benefits of this type of music are:

- improved test scores;
- a cut in learning time;
- the calming of hyperactive children;

- reduction in errors;
- an improvement in creativity and clarity;
- integration of both sides of the brain for more efficient learning;
- raised IQ scores.

In the US the College Entrance Exam Board Service conducted a study on all students taking their SAT exams. For those students who sang or played a musical instrument, a score of 51 points higher out of a total of 800 points on the verbal portion of the test and 39 points higher out of a total of 800 points on the maths section of the test was achieved.

In the world of work, forty-two of the world's largest corporations such as Shell, IBM and Dupont use certain Baroque pieces to cut learning time and increase retention of knowledge of new material. Creativity apparently also soars when exposed to this type of music. Indeed, Dupont used a music listening programme in one department that cut its training time in half and doubled the number of people trained. Another corporation found that clerical errors decreased by one-third.

Perhaps the most startling effects of Baroque music can be found by examining the work of Dr Georgi Lazonov, a renowned Bulgarian psychologist. He developed a methodology of teaching foreign languages that used Baroque music with a beat pattern of sixty beats per minute. He has demonstrated that in a single day, one-half of the normal vocabulary and phrases for the term had been learnt (up to 1,000 words or phrases). In addition it was claimed that students had an average 92 per cent retention rate.

He has proven conclusively that by using certain Baroque pieces, foreign languages can be mastered with 85–100 per cent effectiveness in thirty days when the usual time is two years. Students who had learnt this way were able to recall this information with nearly 100 per cent accuracy after four years! Any Mozart or Baroque music of about sixty beats per minute allows students to feel calmer, study longer and have a higher rate of retention.

It activates the right and left hemispheres of the brain for the maximum learning potential, a minimum of five times according to the research. There is so much research going on to prove the effects of music that a website has also been created just to keep track of all the new developments called 'MuSica' (see 'Where next?' section for details). There are some who claim that the effects of listening to music have been overstated and misinterpreted. If listening to Mozart can have healing benefits as well, how come Mozart spent most of his life ill?! However, from a teacher's point of view this needn't be a problem.

Take this scenario: the classroom teacher explains to the class that they should listen to some Mozart while they are busy completing their written assignments. He goes on to say that the reason for this is that if they listen carefully to the music it will deliver the benefit of increasing their intellectual abilities. As the teacher plays the music he notices a shift in the atmosphere of the room to one where the pupils in the class are fairly quiet, more focused on their task and not easily distracted. At a pre-arranged time the class are asked to stop writing and the CD is turned off. Does it actually matter to the class or the classroom teacher whether or not exposure to Mozart has or has not affected their intellectual capacity? This situation has in fact become a self-fulfilling prophecy. Tell the class what will happen and they will think it has. Has any harm been done? The teacher thinks not. He notices how much more settled the class were than normal. This encouraged them to be more accurate and focused. This may well be what improved the quality of their work, not 'the Mozart effect'.

Some of the other uses of music might be:

- Classical music can be a pleasing way to drown out the distraction that can come from 'white noise'. Examples might be noisy central heating, noisy classrooms that are located nearby, external noise particularly if your classroom is close to the edge of the school campus near roads and public transport routes.

- Classical music is a good choice to play perhaps while pupils are taking tests or timed written assignments. This can support the brain falling into the 'alpha brain wave' state. A condition described as 'relaxed alertness' that is the optimum one for learning. When under hypnosis for example the brain falls into 'delta brain wave' state, which may or may not be the optimum one for a teacher to achieve with pupils!
- If for no other reason, it may develop an appreciation of a music form that might ordinarily be alien to the pupils.

Lighting and temperature

In many schools it is often difficult to command effective control over the heating and lighting situation in a classroom. However, for those who find their rooms consistently well heated and well lit it is important to recognise the observations made in the Dunn and Dunn Learning Style Inventory in Chapter 1. Some pupils will thrive in a very warm classroom, others will prefer to be able to feel much cooler. Similarly, a well lit or dimly lit room will variously suit different pupils at different times. The message for teacher is to vary the temperature (not to either extreme though!) and luminosity of rooms.

As a general rule however, pupils will be most alert in rooms that are on the cool side, perhaps in the low seventies (degrees Fahrenheit). It may be necessary to open as many doors and windows as possible to create a cool air flow particularly in the summer months. Plants are a way of making a room welcoming but also improve the air quality, particularly in air-conditioned rooms.

* * *

Any endeavours that are made to improve the classroom environment should be shared with as many of the pupils as possible. It is clear that once the imperfection of the learning environment is shared with pupils and improvements identified, there is a corresponding improvement in the attitude and motivation of students to learn. The next section, 'In the classroom' offers a way to make this happen in the classroom.

IN THE CLASSROOM

If you want your classroom to become an enriched learning environment, here is a checklist to start the process.

Display

- Create dedicated wall space for pupils' work that is double-mounted and of high quality. Encourage pupils to take ownership and authority over this space. Create a rota for pupils to help mount and display work, changing it every six to eight weeks.
- Suggest a set of rules that govern the quality of display space, such as colours, double-mounting, ICT-generated titles, balance between written and visual, which pupils' work, which year groups and which topics to display.
- Identify dedicated wall space that is used for work that is related to content. This display work should be legible from anywhere in the room and be in the peripheral vision of all pupils. It should identify key learning content. Again, change this every six to eight weeks.
- Encourage older students, perhaps with graphic arts/ICT expertise, to support the production of display work.
- If the display space appears old and shabby, invest in paint to create an attractive backdrop. Use bold and bright colours such as blues, greens and reds.

Case study 5.1

Creating a school display policy:

1   All departments agree to make 'Display' an item on department meeting agendas as well as in any development planning documentation.

2   All departments are asked to nominate an amount of money they feel they need to fund this drive to improve displays around school.

3   All areas of the school that have display space (classrooms, corridors, foyers) are to have a designated person responsible for that space.

4   A commitment to changing displays every six to eight weeks will be undertaken by all people responsible for these spaces.

5   A combination of commercial and pupil-created work should form the basis of the displays.

6   Departmental colour schemes should be adopted to create some sense of 'corporate' image.

7   All pupil work should be that pupil's best effort. However, where possible the work should meet whole school standards on spelling and presentation.

8   The school administration team have agreed to offer administrative help to subjects on a rota basis to provide help and support in creating displays.

9   Display work should be inspirational and aspirational wherever possible.

10   Incidents of damage and abuse to display areas should be treated decisively and rectified immediately.

11   Displays should be relevant, lively and stimulating.

Creating a school policy that has the shared issue of improving the visual environment of the school in an effort to raise the sense of ownership and belonging to all members of the school community, is something everyone can gain from.

Music

There are a number of ways that the teacher can begin the process of utilising the benefits of music in the classroom. For example:

- If you have access to a school intranet system, download Baroque music (Vivaldi, Bach and Handel) on to it. This can then be played through speakers that are plugged into a networked PC in the classroom. It becomes a permanent resource that is easily and quickly accessible for both the students and the teacher, from anywhere in the school, with multiple access, all done simultaneously.
- Consider buying a number of classical music CDs that can be loaned out to pupils who work at home.
- Extol the virtues of listening to radio stations that are dedicated to classical music while completing homework or other out of school learning.
- Share with students the potential benefit of listening to classical music as a way of increasing the chances of it becoming an accepted and regular feature in learning.
- Consider the broad use of music in learning to not only help concentration levels and attention but also to signal a break/change in activity or to greet/dismiss pupils to and from the lesson.

Case study 5.2

The maths department want to develop the use of music in the classroom but want to use it for a variety of purposes. A number of colleagues had done some research on which types of music fit which purpose best. It seemed sensible to initially buy Mozart's 'Sonata for Two Pianos in D Major'. This is the piece of music that caused a sell-out in the US as it benefited maths students when they listened to it prior to taking a test. As the teachers all agreed that expertise in classical music was not their strength, they were thankful that they had worked with the school's specialist music teacher who had offered some helpful comments on some of the pieces. They decided to have music that would fit the following purposes, so chose the following:

Beginnings of lessons as pupils enter the class:
Beethoven 'Symphony No. 5 in E Minor – Allegro con brio'
Prokoviev 'Montagues and Capulets' from 'Romeo and Juliet'
Handel 'Hallelujah Chorus' from the 'Messiah' (the best-known oratorio ever written)

Creating a mood:
Elgar 'Cello Concerto in E Minor. Adagio – moderato' (powerful and uplifting)
Holst 'The Planets – Jupiter Suite' (rousing)
Albinoni 'Adagio in G Minor' (haunting)

Music for energising:
Rossini 'William Tell Overture' (gets them going!)
Vivaldi 'The Four Seasons' (popular and likely to be well known)
Elgar 'Pomp and Circumstance'

Music for relaxing:
Debussy 'Clair de Lune' (atmospheric)
Mozart 'Concert for Flute and Harp in II Andantino' (serene)
Vaughan Williams 'Fantasia on a Theme by Thomas Tallis' (evocative)

Background music to hide 'white noise':
Mike Oldfield 'Tubular Bells' (popular)
Jean Michel Jarre 'Equinoxe' (ideal as background)
Vangelis 'Love Theme' taken from the film *Bladerunner*

End of lessons to review learning:
Mozart 'Concerto No. 21 in C Major – Andante'
Bach 'Orchestral Suite No. 3 in D – Air on the G String'
Vivaldi 'Flute Concerto No. 3 in D Major – Cantabile'

The department agreed to download the music on to the school's intranet so that it would be accessible from any of the school's classroom, networked computers. It also meant other subjects could access the music too if they wanted to. The pupils also had the opportunity to listen to this music while completing independent learning assignments from any networked computers around the school. All this could be done simultaneously.

Light

Ordinarily it is important for classrooms to be well lit. However, at times it is appropriate to make the room as dark as possible. The Dunn and Dunn Learning Style Inventory (Chapter 1) indicates that some learners prefer dimly lit spaces for some of the time. The teacher should recognise this possibility and also that a dimly lit room helps create a mood. It also improves clarity to LCD and video work.

Layout

As mentioned in the section 'Theoretical background', changing the layout of the classroom can have a beneficial effect for no other reason than the novelty of the situation creates a lasting impression on the long-term memory. The layout of a room also has the potential to affect the behaviour of pupils for good and bad. However, a change in layout is also important to allow a specific activity to work more effectively. The following is a simple exercise to highlight the range of possibilities

On a piece of paper draw fifteen tables and thirty chairs and cut them out. Now on a larger piece of paper representing the classroom, arrange these in at least ten different ways and suggest what kinds of activities suit certain layouts. There are a number of possible variations shown below.

'Horseshoe'

Lay the tables in the shape of a horseshoe or a U shape. It may be that you are left with three or four tables, if so, arrange these as a group of three in the middle of the room. This arrangement allows the teacher to achieve a number of things. All the class can be seen and are looking the same way, so supporting management of the pupils. It creates a lot of space to the front of the classroom allowing the teacher to set up electronic equipment such as an LCD projector, overhead projector or video, offering clear viewing for all pupils. This arrangement also affords the opportunity to locate all resources and materials for the lesson centrally on a 'resource island'. The area at the front also allows space for pupils to perform role-plays or demonstrations.

'Circles'

Move all the tables to one side of the room and place the chairs in a circle. This is an excellent layout for active and engaging activities. Examples of this might be 'Chinese whispers'. The idea is that content is reviewed through the pupil whispering one statement to their partner. This is then passed on to next person by a whisper together with an additional piece of information. It is possible to do this in a number of ways. Keeping the groups smaller in number means that the number of separate pieces of information one pupil needs to process can be reduced. In any event the idea is that the amount of knowledge builds up. The person at the end of the circle then shares all the group's separate pieces of knowledge. In 'Chinese whispers' the idea is that errors are made and in the same way the group then corrects errors that are made when all the separate pieces of information are shared.

'Fours'

Perhaps one of the most effective ways of improving learning for boys and girls is to sit two boys and two girls in tables of four pupils. This group work situation works very well for problem-solving, investigation and 'making' activities. It allows the teacher a lot of movement around the class, although the teacher will not necessarily be able to see all the pupils' faces all of the time. This requires the teacher to be moving around the class all the time to shift the focus of pupils' attentions. This is particularly important when bringing the class to order or when reviewing learning or checking understanding.

'Rows'

No doubt the easiest layout to support behaviour management is having the pupils facing the front in rows, though this restricts teacher access and movement around the room. It also works against incorporating problem-solving, active and enquiry-based learning situations.

*   *   *

Figure 5.1 represents one possible layout, together with its strengths and weaknesses.

Strengths

- This layout offers the flexibility for the teacher and pupils not only to move fairly freely around the classroom, but also to locate resources and foci of the lesson at different points.
- Access to the 'resource island' equipped with all the necessary resources for the lesson ensures pupils do not obscure vision of the white board.
- The position of the teacher's desk is in an unconventional location. This is deliberate. The idea is to shift the emphasis away from a traditional set up. Access to the white board for any interactive activities is unrestricted and it allows the front part of the classroom to be a focus for learning rather than a 'bolt hole' for the teacher.

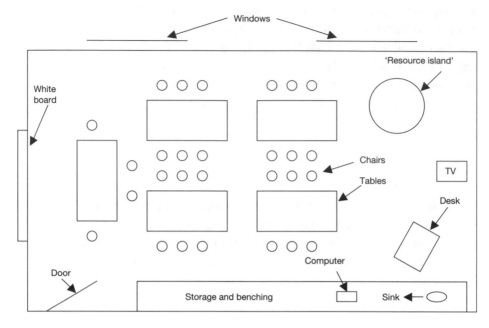

Figure 5.1 Effective classroom layout

- Pupils' desks are not located next to the wall. This is so that there is less opportunity for graffiti or damage to displays.
- Apart from the white board this classroom has no obvious front or back. Indeed, this layout offers the opportunity for learning to be focused on various points of the classroom. For example, a flip chart could be located by the teacher's desk. Part of the lesson could focus on material and stimuli on the flip chart. Similarly, this is an excellent location for short extracts of video work. Other parts of the lesson could be focused on the white board at the front. Focusing on displays as learning tools for the lesson is also possible.
- The desks at the front allow pupils with sight issues to be closer to the white board.
- The desks are broadly concentrated to the middle of the room. This is to restrict the amount of 'glare' that can be a problem as the lighting can reflect off the white board for pupils sitting to the far sides of the room.

- Tables of six allow for collaborative, problem-solving, investigative learning. It also allows for more creative activities that require a degree of space and room for cutting, gluing or sticking.
- Tables of six also free up more access for easier movement and more floor space.
- The seating arrangement also allows for the pupils to easily shift their focus from one side of the room to the other without completely having to turn around.
- The area at the opposite end to the white board provides room for demonstrations or mini role-plays.
- Groupings of six allow for greater gender integration in seating arrangements. This allows girls and boys to not only learn from each others' strengths but also support each others' weaknesses.
- Improved classroom management may also be possible through managing the seating arrangements of individuals who do not work productively together.
- Groupings of six may also provide greater opportunity to seat pupils who share similar learning style profiles. For example, seating kinaesthetic learners together. There may also be the added benefit of offering greater efficiency in the use of supplies. For example, the scissors, glue and paint may only be required on some of the tables as the others may be populated with, for example, intrapersonal or reflective learners.

Weaknesses

- Tables of six may create too much of a temptation for pupils to engage in 'off-task' chatter.
- The teacher may feel that classroom problems are exacerbated by pupils being able to look at each other too much and not being able to focus on the teacher enough.

Case study 5.3

The geography department is looking forward to welcoming a new colleague who will be starting work in September. Fortunately she will be able to work in her own room for 90 per cent of the week. The head of department is anxious for her to feel that she 'owns' the room and offers a checklist/wish-list for her to consider so that she can create the learning space she wants:

- Is the lighting appropriate and functioning correctly?
- Is the environment free of unnecessary distractions?
- Is the seating situation appropriate (number and condition of chairs)?
- How should I organise the tables/desks?
- Are there areas of the room that may become too congested and access difficult?
- Are entrances to the classroom located in such a way as to minimise distraction?
- Should I have a dedicated resource area?
- Should I have a dedicated 'resource island'?
- Should I identify a reading/reflection/independent study area?
- How easily will I be able to move around the room?
- How should I design the walls?
- What kinds of posters should I have (informational, expectations, motivational, humorous)?
- How I should I manage/locate/utilise music?
- Do I like the colour of the walls and can I do anything about it?

The idea is that this checklist becomes an 'aide-mémoire' for the new appointment to use so that the issue of the importance of the classroom environment remains at the forefront of her thinking.

The classroom environment is something we have a lot of control over. We should make the benefits of a high-quality classroom clear to budget holders and policy makers in our schools. There are resource implications for some of what has preceded but overall the costs are relatively minor. The real challenge is a change in approach to how we see this 'silent helper'.

*   *   *

The next section, 'Where next?' offers further references to develop a deeper understanding of some of the research background, in particular, to neurological advances into how our understanding of environmental factors impacts on learning.

WHERE NEXT?

The impetus for this chapter came from the work of Marian Diamond, a neuro-atomist in the Department of Integrative Biology at the University of California, Berkeley. It was her work on the how the brain responds to enrichment that has prompted the debate about how the brain actually changes in response to certain external stimuli. She is author of more than a hundred scientific articles and three books including *Magic Trees of the Mind* and *Enriching Hereditary*. For a more detailed overview of her work there is an excellent website www.newhorizons.org that has among other things many links to developments in the neurosciences generally and their application in the classroom.

The impacts of displays on long-term recall are more fully explored in two books by Eric Jensen, *Super Teaching* and *Environments for Learning*. The latter book reinforces the notion that there is no such thing as a 'neutral' learning environment and that, in fact, the classroom will either work with or against the learner. As mentioned earlier in this chapter, there are many websites devoted to music and the effects on learning such as the dedicated website on research related to the effects of music on the brain www. MuSica.com or www.mozarteffect.com. Perhaps one of the most popular books on the topic of the effects of classical music is Don Campbell's *The Mozart Effect.*

For a more detailed overview on the impact of colour on the brain, there are a number of colour therapy websites (such as www. colour-therapy.com) that extol the benefits of a carefully managed colour environment. Similarly the largely ignored effects of smell can be more fully developed through websites (such as www. macalester.edu/~psych/whathap/UBNRP/Smell/memory.html).

Conclusion

What are the five steps to accelerate learning in the classroom and how does a teacher plan this? There are a number of variables present when learning is not only good but when pupils are learning more quickly and understanding more deeply than 'normal'. This is accelerated learning. The optimum planning model to achieve this is not the traditional linear one but, rather, a holistic one.

The following twenty-point checklist should provide an aide-mémoire for you:

Learning

1 Carry out a learning style questionnaire for pupils.
2 Carry out a pupil audit on how they prefer to learn.
3 Examine your own methodology and honestly reflect on the range of learning styles used.
4 Identify three key references for further reading.

Cognition

5   Select a repertoire of activities from the seven intelligences and incorporate into planning.
6   Carry out a Multiple Intelligence audit on the pupils.
7   Identify types of thinking skill challenges evidenced through planning.
8   Ensure the whole range of challenges can be met.

Gender

9   Reflect on learning characteristics of boys and girls with reference to their strengths and weaknesses.
10   Select a range of activities to suit natural strengths and weaknesses of boys and girls and build this into planning.
11   Plan a range of commands to match differentiated abilities.
12   Audit opinions of boys and girls on factors that improve/ mitigate effective learning.

Whole lesson

13   Plan a range of tasks to begin lessons.
14   Plan a range of tasks to end lessons.
15   Ask pupils to memorise key content and share 'stories' they used to memorise facts.
16   Record reading speeds before and after teaching speed-reading strategies.

Physical environment

17   Change classroom peripherals to become more visual and learner friendly.
18   Change seating arrangements regularly to fit purpose.
19   Experiment with use of music for different purposes.
20   Discuss with pupils the use of managing the smells of the classroom!

Use this checklist when planning what you are going to do with your pupils. Each chapter has a repertoire of methods and ideas that can be used with your classes. Of course not all of them will be appropriate for all your classes. When you don't know your class well, there are questionnaires to help you get a closer look at their learning profiles. At other times your experience and that of others will help you formulate what is most appropriate.

However, it is vitally important that you think flexibly and imaginatively when thinking about how to use this book with your pupils. Some of the ideas discussed will both challenge and support your work in the classroom. Sometimes a 'step change' in how you view your work in the classroom can be healthy. For example, a lesson that uses finger puppets can be appropriate for A-level students as well as for the class of five-year-olds where I first saw them used!

Above all do not work in isolation. Share your ideas and thoughts with your pupils. Explain why you want to do the things you are proposing. Express your hopes and concerns. Make it a collaborative exercise. You will be amazed at the positive relationships that can be developed with this degree of honesty.

This book should inspire and inform in a way that leads you to reflect on your work in the classroom but above all allows you to remind yourself of how it feels to be someone who can change lives through the power of learning. Something, after all, that brought you to work in the classroom in the first place.

Bibliography

Arnold, R., *Raising Levels of Achievement in Boys*, Slough: National Foundation for Educational Research, 1997.

Bandler, R. and Grindler, J., *Frogs into Princes – Neuro Linguistic Programming*, California: NLP Comprehensive, 1979.

Baron-Cohen, S., *The Essential Difference – The Truth About the Male and Female Brain*, New York: Perseus Publishing, 2003.

Bennett, N., *Teaching Style and Pupil Progress*, London: Open Books, 1976.

Birren, F., *Colour and Human Response*, New York: Van Nostrand Rheinhold, 1984.

Bloom, B., *Taxonomy of Educational Objectives*, New York: David Mackay, 1956.

Blum, D., *Sex on the Brain*, London: Penguin Books, 1998.

Briggs, K.C. and Myers, I.B., *Myers–Briggs Type Indicator*, Palo Alto, CA: Davies–Black Publishing, 1997.

Briggs-Myers, I. and Myers, P., *Gifts Differing – Understanding Personality Type*, Palo Alto, CA: Davies–Black Publishing, 1995.

Brookfield, D., *Developing Critical Thinkers*, Buckingham: Open University Press, 1987.

Bruner, J., *Towards a Theory of Instruction*, Cambridge, MA: Harvard University Press, 1966.

Buzan, T., *The Mind Map Book*, New York: Plume Books, 1996.

Caine, R.N. and Caine, G., *Making Connections: Teaching and the Human Brain*, Alexandria, VA: ASCD, 1991.

Calvin, W., *How Brains Think: Evolving Intelligence Then and Now*, New York: Basic Books, 1997.

Campbell, D., *Introduction to the Musical Brain*, Texas: Richardson, 1983.

Campbell, K., *Teaching and Learning through Multiple Intelligences*, Needham Heights, MA: Allyn and Bacon, 1996.

Chandler, S. and Leat, D., *Thinking through Geography*, Cambridge: Chris Kingston Publishing, 1998.

Collins, J. and Cook, D., *Understanding Learning: Influences and Outcomes*, London: Paul Chapman, 2000.

Cooper, P. and McIntyre, D., *Effective Teaching and Learning: Teachers' and Students' Perspectives*, Buckingham: Open University Press, 1996.

Diamond, M., *Enriching Hereditary: The Impact of the Environment on the Anatomy of the Brain*, New York: Free Press, 1988.

Diamond, M., *Magic Trees of the Mind*, New York: Plume Books, 1999.

Dunn, R. and Dunn, K., *Teaching Secondary Students through their Individual Learning Styles*, Boston: Allyn and Bacon, 1993.

Fisher, R., *Teaching Children to Think*, London: Blackwell, 1991.

Fisher, R., *Teaching Children to Learn*, London: Stanley Thornes, 1995.

Gardner, H., *Frames of Mind: The Theory of Multiple Intelligences*, London: Fontana, 1993.

Gregorc, A.F., *Gregorc Style Delineator*, Connecticut: Gregorc Associates Inc., 1984.

Gregorc, A.F., *Inside Styles: Beyond the Basics*, Maynard, MA: Gabriel Systems Inc., 1985.

Higbee, K., *Your Memory – How it Works and How to Improve it*, New York: Marlowe, 1996.

Jensen, E., *The Learning Brain*, Del Mar, CA: Turning Point, 1994.

Jensen, E., *Brain-based Learning and Teaching*, Del Mar, CA: Turning Point, 1995.

Jensen, E., *Environments for Learning*, Del Mar, CA: Turning Point, 1995.

Jensen, E., *Completing the Puzzle: A Brain-based Approach to Learning*, Del Mar, CA: Turning Point, 1996.

Joyce, B., Calhoun, E. and Hopkins, D., *Models of Learning – Tools for Teaching*, Buckingham: Open University Press, 1997.

Jung, C., *The Four Basic Psychological Functions of Man and the Establishment of Uniformities in Human Structures*, American Institute of Psychological Research, 1984.

Kimura, D., *Sex and Cognition*, Colorado: Bradford Books, 2000.

Kolb, D., *Experiential Learning – Experience as a Source of Learning and Development*, Financial Times Prentice Hall, 1983.

Kotulak, R., *Inside the Brain*, Kansas City, MO: Andrews and McMeel, 1996.

Lazear, D., *Seven Ways of Teaching: The Artistry of Teaching with Multiple Intelligences*, Arizona: Zephyr Press, 1993.

Marshall, L., *Discoveries in the Human Brain: Neuroscience Prehistory, Brain Structure and Function*, Totowa, NJ: Humana Press, 1998.

Moir, A. and Jessel, D., *Brain Sex*, McHenry, IL: Delta, 1992.

Nisbet, J. and Shucksmith, J., *Learning Strategies*, London: Routledge, 1986.

Ornstein, R., *The Right Mind: Making Sense of the Hemispheres*, New York: Harcourt Brace, 1997.

Pinker, S., *How the Mind Works*, London: Norton and Co., 1998.

Ranson, S., *Towards the Learning Society*, London: Cassell, 1994.

Rose, C. and Goll, L., *Accelerate Your Learning*, Accelerated learning systems, 1992.

Rose, S., *The Making of Memory*, London: Bantam Press, 1993.

Shipman, M., *In Search of Learning*, Oxford: Blackwell, 1990.

Smith, A., *Accelerated Learning in the Classroom*, Stafford: Network Educational Press Ltd, 1996.

Sylwester, R., *A Celebration of Neurons*, Alexandria, VA: ASCD, 1995.

Vygotsky, L.S., *Mind in Society: The Development of Higher Psychological Processes*, Cambridge, MA: Harvard University Press, 1978.

Wenger, W., *The Einstein Factor*, Rocklin, CA: Prima Publishing, 1996.

Index

Please note that page references to non-textual information such as Figures and Boxes are in *italic* print